RISE
A Call to the Light Tribe

CYNTHIA GOMEZ

Light Rising Publishing

Rise: A Call to the Light Tribe
Copyright © 2021 by Cynthia Gomez

All rights reserved. No part of this book may be reproduced, distributed, or transmitted in any printed or electronic form, without the prior written permission of the author, except for certain noncommercial uses permitted by copyright law. For permission requests, contact Light Rising Publishing.

Light Rising Publishing
www.lightrisingpublishing.com

Design & Layout
Cynthia Gomez
Light Rising Publishing

Print ISBN 978-1-7328238-5-3
Printed in the United States of America.

Dedication

To all the teachers, helpers, and guardian angels now beyond the veil who have graced my path, thank you for lifting me up, inspiring me, and lighting the way forward. Sir Lancelot, for showing me how to be in this world; Aileen for picking me up when I fell; and too many others to name—may blessings always rain down upon your heads and may you always walk in light. And for the team that remains—those earthly points of light walking the walk and fighting the fight—you are not alone. We've got this.

Table of Contents

Dedication	iii
Preface	vii
Part 1. Stepping into Our Roles	1
Chapter 1. The Time is Now	3
Chapter 2. The Magic of Breaking	17
Chapter 3. Walking the Cobbled Road	26
Chapter 4. Spiraling Upwards	40
Part 2. Transcendence in A Broken World	44
Chapter 5. The Fear Trap	45
Chapter 6. Taking Stock	56
Part 3. The War for Our Minds	64
Chapter 7. The Weaponization of Words	65
Chapter 8. Becoming Guardians of Truth	71
Part 4. We're Who We've Been Waiting For	93
Chapter 9. Laying Our Old Selves to Rest	94
Chapter 10. Emerging from the Chrysalis	101
Chapter 11. The Great Work Ahead	105
About the Author	113

Preface

*E*verything in this book has already been said in many different places and in many different ways. Nothing I say is new, but I say it because, for almost as long as I can remember, the universe has been tugging gently at the edges of my consciousness like a small child pulling sheepishly at mom's shirt as if to say, "there's something I need you to do." And I knew I would do it since I was a child; I came here to do it.

But why sit to write things already written? Because the lens sometimes is everything, and I hope the lens through which I've filtered the information on these pages is exactly the lens you need to remember yourself and why you're here. This book represents a combination of the knowledge with which I came into this body, woven with information acquired over a lifetime's study of "soul science," the intersection of spirituality with every branch of knowledge; a lifelong passion for epistemology, the philosophy of truth; and the wisdom of my lived dharma. Some of it may resonate deeply, and some may feel entirely foreign. Take what serves you and

RISE: A CALL TO THE LIGHT TRIBE

leave the rest, but be willing for the sake of your own remembrance to sit with that which makes you squirm, for truth is not always comforting, convenient, or congruent with our programming. Allow yourself to be challenged, and to shine a light into the dark spaces. It is safe to do so. A more whole, future you stands at your rear in support of this evolving current you.

Ram Dass once said "I am not a teacher; I am a reflection of you through which information flows to you from source, and you teach me as I teach you." So open your mind wider than you have ever before, and know that everything I say to you, I say to myself.

As our paths collide in your picking up this book, remember that all paths are paths. One does not necessarily invalidate another, but may actually add context if we are willing to see out our windshields from different lanes of the same superhighway. There is no need to throw away one belief system because another suddenly seems to fit too. They are just different ways through which to see universal truth. Discard the man-made dogma and find the commonalities. Honor the diversity of the oneness.

In writing this, I honor my path. I am here not to teach, but to extend a hand to those seeking to reconnect with the light grid from which we came and to which we will return, as instruments of the universal realization of "as above, so below." This book is a call to remembrance of your perfection and purpose. I seek not to persuade you of anything; only to ring the bell of remembrance.

In times of encroaching darkness, we must emerge from our own confusion and the forgetfulness of this grand illusion to shine the world into sacred balance. This is what we signed up for, and the time is now. We are the creators of tomorrow.

Join me,

Cynthia Gomez

Part 1
Stepping into Our Roles

Chapter 1
The Time is Now

*Y*ou are more powerful than you might imagine. You have not only the power to transform your life how you see fit, but also to play a role in birthing a New Earth. You are a co-creator of your reality and of mine, and I write this to awaken you to your power, for it is needed. Now is the time. I invite you to rise with me in light.

You know who you are, the light workers, the star blossoms, the awakening earth souls; the ones who have always felt a vague sense of distinct purpose. It's growing stronger, isn't it? Clearer. We are here to help Gaia through this cycle of rebirth as we ourselves ascend into greater integration with our multidimensional selves. You know this. You have probably always sensed this.

I knew I would write this book since the age of 11, I just didn't know quite how. Not until everything fell apart—until I fell apart. It was not until my own blessed destruction that the words poured forth as I began again, like a caterpillar recreating itself into a butterfly from its own liquefied remains or a phoenix taking shape from the ashes even as the fire burned. So I spent the first part of my life learning through study so much of what I innately already knew.

No doubt, it is a difficult time and place to be alive. Suffering is rampant as all around us, old paradigms based on separation create wealth for a tiny minority while the rest suffer and Gaia's resources are exhausted at a record pace. We are witnessing a never-experienced convergence of distinct but interrelated cycles; economies, climate change, and conflict cycles are all simultaneously coming to a head as Earth's magnetic poles reverse. But as the ground shifts under us and old paradigms based on separation and greed crumble, we are reminded that this is exactly what we signed up for. We are the cleanup crew and the recovery team, ready and equipped to re-imagine and rebuild a better world in the wake of what's left as antiquated systems begin to fall away.

We came here as a team with a divine directive of anchoring the light grid, and we are in for quite a show. It's important to remember this—that we are here now of our own volition, and that we have a supremely important job to do. I know you know this—as I do—with inexplicable certainty that has always been as much a core part of you as the marrow of your bones. We are a species with amnesia, yet our individual remembering is meant to trigger a collective remembering. It has already begun. My goal is to provide some guidance for how we accomplish what we came into these bodies to do, despite the limitations of the dense, three-dimensional matrix into which we have incarnated.

Wise beings in ancient times wrote about the Precession of the Equinoxes, a process that modern astronomy has only rediscovered

CHAPTER 1. THE TIME IS NOW

in the past several hundred years. The prevailing theory describes the near-26,000-year cycle it takes the earth to complete a full "wobble" on its axis, which coincides with the amount of time it takes for all the constellations to seemingly rotate around the earth. Much like a spinning top, Earth points away from the center of the galaxy for nearly 13,000 years, and then towards it for close to another 13,000 years in a semi-counterclockwise motion. One way to visualize the precession is as an oblong shape with a length greater than its height. The end of 2012 marked the beginning of the end of movement backwards, placing us right below the turn and moving upward. We now find ourselves smack in the middle of that turn, and about to begin picking up forward momentum.

A second theory—a binary star model—posits that Earth doesn't really wobble on its axis, but rather only appears to do so to the earthbound observer as a result on the earth's orbit around the sun while the sun apparently orbits a third mass (a companion star), and the entire solar system moves relative to the galactic sun in an oscillating wave pattern. Regardless which theory you subscribe to, the result is still Precession.

The Mayans, master astrologers, called the galactic center "Hunab Ku," referring to it as the ultimate creator of everything in our Galaxy through bursts of consciousness energy. This energy informs everything. As we receive energy more directly from the Milky Way's galactic center, we are decoding it, some more consciously than others. This is the impetus, many believe, for the spiritual and physical evolution we are now seeing among all living things. As we move with the galactic winds described by ancient Sanskrit writings, we begin to wake up. Each time beings on this planet find themselves at this point in the precession, they wake up a bit more than the previous cycle before falling back into slumber.

RISE: A CALL TO THE LIGHT TRIBE

Simultaneously, the sun's position on the vernal equinox, which happens in March, moves into a new constellation roughly every 2,150 years. Currently, we are at the cusp between the Age of Pisces—of religious belief, dogma, and clashes of ideology—and the Age of Aquarius—of recognizing that all paths are paths, and of a more inclusive spirituality. The Mayans thought of this time as passing through the "galactic underworld," a transitional period of chaotic changes and unveiling universal truths. Indeed, the changes have been coming hard and fast.

We have never woken up to this degree. This ultimate Age of Aquarius brings with it a new way of being, for all of us, including Gaia. This is a time of geophysical transformation. Scientists tell us this is true, and we can see it with our own eyes. This is where we are, participants to a mass awakening, remembering that we came here lead the way out of darkness. As humankind collectively wakes up, we are becoming less matter-based and more light-based beings, with increased capacity for learning at the soul level without the need to suffer our lessons.

To become the bringers of a New Earth, we must both be in alignment with our purpose and have the resources we need to carry out that purpose. While struggle has much to teach us, the time for struggle must end so that we can step into our roles from a place of loving abundance—one that offers more sustainability to both us as individuals and to Gaia as a whole. This is the greatest awakening yet, and it may very well be our last chance to save ourselves from a destruction of our own making.

The Japanese Zen tradition teaches that human beings learn in one of two distinct ways. The first, "kensho" involves pain. The second, "satori," is growth through insight. At lower densities, kensho learning is more common. But as we awaken and connect to the information that is always all around us, "satori" becomes increasingly available to us. The key then, is to embrace practices that allow us to access that information.

That is not to say that we can avoid pain altogether. Struggle often results from karmic debts and soul contracts designed to help us grow. Humans are materially dense creatures who learn best through experience. Because we hurt others, we must experience pain ourselves. And we do hurt others, despite our best intentions. Our first act as a human, in fact, is to rip through our mother's insides on our way from the womb into this reality. Yet, here we are, at a unique point in history, with the opportunity to awaken in this dream, to become more than human, and to transcend the karmic cycle of suffering.

Do the difficult inner work of looking deeply into the mirror and bringing light to the darkest corners of your inner world. Learn your lessons. As we heal ourselves, the world heals a little more. Through healing, we can sidestep the cycle of further suffering while simultaneously stepping into our power as master creators of a reality that is better aligned with our souls' purpose.

Manifesting is the art of tuning into the void, unified field, or ether—whatever your preferred terminology—where one might see nothing, but where pure potential exists—to direct the materialization of that potential. Much has been written about manifesting, and although this is not exactly a book about personal manifesting, the many components of successful manifestation are coincidentally the very same that will help us embody divine light.

We pass through darkness so that we may see our own light, and light the way for those behind us still stumbling in the dark. In inviting you to take my hand and walk alongside me, I do my

RISE: A CALL TO THE LIGHT TRIBE

part to strengthen the light grid by empowering you to shine as only you can for those whose lives you touch. We are instruments of the universe, called for nearly 13,000 years to surrender to the creative void of darkness—to create ourselves from that darkness, so that we may switch on as the time of light arrives. End the resistance to being who and what you are, using your energy to align your own creative urges with the glimmers of New Earth. Our manifesting is accelerated when we manifest for greater good, for others as much as ourselves.

And it must be so, that we move not only with precision, but also with speed, towards our purpose-driven goals. We must keep up. You may sense that time is speeding up as you become someone and something other than who and what you were, or perhaps entirely who and what you were before your human programming. From a biological standpoint, it is a well-documented phenomenon that we perceive time as going by faster as we age, sort of like gaining momentum as we race towards that doorway that marks our departure from an embodied existence and reentry into the world of spirit.

You may be shaking your head, thinking, "no, that can't be it." So, let me add to that. The world's scientific timekeepers have recently proposed shortening the minute to 59 seconds as the earth's orbit around the sun speeds up. In a very concrete way then, we are experiencing a quickening. Let's not stop here, though. The world of physics accepts that time is relative. The effect of "gravitational time dilation" states that the stronger the gravity of an object, the more space-time curves, and the slower time goes. Physics has established that time passes faster at the top of a mountain than at the bottom. Consider then, the claim that we are moving into lighter densities and operating at higher

CHAPTER 1. THE TIME IS NOW

frequencies, and what this may mean in terms of the passage of time. Let's not stop there, though. The rate of precession is accelerating, while at the same time the Schumann resonance, a global electromagnetic resonance sometimes likened as Gaia's heartbeat, has been rising.

While any causal relationship between these things remains unclear, what is clear is that a lot is happening, both within and outside us, resulting in changes not just in our bodies and world, but also in our perception.

It is a slow but accelerating fall towards the singularity. Allow me explain. At the center of our galaxy sits a supermassive black hole called Sagittarius A, its mass roughly four million times our sun. Like every living thing, it is enclosed by a toroidal energy field shaped much like a donut. The singularity is a one-dimensional, infinitely small space inside of black holes where gravity and density are infinite, and where space-time curves infinitely. Here, the laws of known physics break down. This is where everything swallowed by a black hole goes, and from which, arguably, it is birthed anew. In a human, the singularity is the place where everything we take from the top of the toroidal field hits the center of our torus and is transformed into part of who we are, including our views and personality.

We are, in a physical and metaphorical sense, constantly re-birthing ourselves in accordance with the information we receive from all sources while also moving towards the singularity of another, inconceivably larger being than ourselves. We are fractal spirits, undergoing transformation along with Gaia, who is also a fractal spirit. As above, so below. As we recreate ourselves, we can allow our vibrational state to inform our material environment to reflect our roles as bringers of New

RISE: A CALL TO THE LIGHT TRIBE

Earth. We can become better inputs for the singularity to which we are all proceeding into, so as to birth something better on the other end. Black holes provide a beautiful metaphor for so much of our lives for so many reasons. They can also teach us about transformative manifestation.

It is now thought that at the center of almost every galaxy lays a supermassive black hole. Black holes can begin as stars, which are born in litters with stars of varying sizes, reminding us that we are all star children, regardless of whether we emit or trap light. Black holes can form when very massive stars reach the end of their life cycle by collapsing into themselves. "Gravitational collapse" results when a star's internal pressure is not enough to resist the object's own gravity. You see, all stars begin by burning hydrogen. They fuse hydrogen atoms, and then helium. Smaller stars can't fuse anything bigger than helium, larger ones continue the process of fusion with heavier elements. While a star's own gravity works to crush the star's mass, the energy released from nuclear fusion creates outward force that prevents a collapse. Stars reach stability when the inward pressure of gravity balances the outward pressure from nuclear fusion.

Once a large star has burned through all the elements up to iron, black hole creation begins. You see, iron is so proton-dense that the fusion process doesn't result in any energy release. It's a dead end, so to speak. Without enough energy from fusion, the force of gravity takes over, and the star's matter crashes down, hits the star's core, and bounces out. This creates an explosion in which the outer layers are blown away—this is a supernova. If what remains is sufficiently massive, gravity essentially just continues to grow, crushing the star's core into a smaller and smaller mass, until it creates a tiny hole in the fabric of space-time.

CHAPTER 1. THE TIME IS NOW

Black holes are everywhere and are being born all the time. They grow by absorbing surrounding masses, including by shredding apart other stars passing close to their event horizon, the invisible boundary from which escape becomes impossible, and whose gravity creates "gravitational lensing," the distortion of light from nearby objects. They can also reach supermassive status by eating smaller black holes and merging with other black holes.

There is another way black holes come to be. Quasars are hungry supermassives, usually found at the centers of galaxies. The spinning in-falling material creates a disk around the edge that is so bright it essentially drowns out the light of the galaxy surrounding it. They are born via a process called "direct collapse," that happens when dense gas clouds collapse from their own gravity. The clouds fragment as the denser parts collapse more quickly than the rest.

In a black hole, gravity is so strong that nothing that enters it can escape. Yet, if you found yourself inside a black hole—and many scientists now believe our galaxy exists within one while also orbiting one—you would see all the light falling in behind you. Eventually, you would reach the singularity, and as some now theorize, would emerge out of the other end as something new from the ingredients of what has been consumed. It is self-actualization on a grand scale.

Does this remind you of a butterfly creating itself from the liquefied remains of a caterpillar within the dark confines of its cocoon? Destruction is a precursor of creation. That is the nature of existence—as much darkness as there is light. Filtered through our linear perception of time, it's a cycle of gain and loss. We gain, and we lose, and we gain and we lose again. But we also gain as we lose and lose as we gain. Like a pendulum in perpetual motion, the universe is always in perfect balance. What seems like a gain is a setup for loss, and what seems like loss is a setup for gain.

This is how it seems as we experience the cycle of life and death and rebirth and all of the spirals within each of those phases of existence. The cycle is both truthful and illusory. We experience joy at the gains and sadness when loss comes. But we fail to see the grander picture as we become caught up in our experiences. The Sanskrit term "maya" refers to the great illusion we must transcend, the veil beyond which the great oneness waits to be discovered. It is, in a pop culture context, the matrix that controls our lives but that is ultimately not as real as that which it conceals.

Nothing is ever truly lost, as everything is transformed and simultaneously transforms us. Every part of every cycle of existence and every swing of the pendulum has purpose. Everything is, and always will be, exactly as it should be. This is what it is to recognize duality and non-duality. We experience the back swing of the pendulum as vastly different than the forward motion, but it's all the same pendulum, doing what a pendulum does, much like the dark and light halves of the yin yang. As everything else, this life is a combination of contradictory, yet intrinsically connected opposites. The point is this: Begin again. You have all of the ingredients you need to re-imagine and rebirth yourself. It is what you were made to do.

But this back swing, man; it's been a weird, rough ride for so many of us, myself included. I understand loss; there's been a lot of it. But you see, while circumstances may seem otherwise, I did this. I am responsible for everything that has come to pass in my

CHAPTER 1. THE TIME IS NOW

life, as are you for everything that you have ever experienced, are now experiencing, and will ever experience. We are the makers of our own realities.

I know this may seem like a callous concept. Life is seemingly chaotic and imperfect, and things often happen that appear to be beyond our control, like illness, natural disasters and random acts of victimization. Some of these events are catastrophic. So, am I saying that some people somehow choose for themselves to be born into abusive situations or with serious impediments, or to die destitute or ravaged by illness? Allow me to clarify.

Humans often like to think of themselves separate from the rest of nature, but we are, like everything around us, pieces of the universe. And like the universe, our souls are on a quest of infinite expansion. We are all tiny gods, creating ourselves as we create the world. In pursuit of expansion, our souls have made contracts in other lives and other dimensions with each other and with our embodied selves to attain certain new knowledge, understanding, and growth, thus arranging situations for our embodied existence that allow us to evolve in that direction. Karmic debts can thus emerge from those contracts.

Life is school for which we all signed up, whether or not we remember that, and suffering is a skilled teacher. You may not have chosen the teacher, but you chose the lesson that needed learning. The suffering is a means to an end. There is randomness, sure, but it's only surface randomness.

This is a hard lesson, and one that requires brutal self-examination and a willingness to shed victimhood and instead accept responsibility for every last action or inaction that has led to the here and now. It requires trusting that what you are experiencing is meant for you. It's also a lesson that changes

RISE: A CALL TO THE LIGHT TRIBE

everything. When you learn to see the matrix for what it is, you can change the code.

I'm not saying it's easy. Waking up to this truth can be a painful, destructive process. When the illusion that life is akin to a leaf blowing in the wind vanishes, life as you know it may shatter because the life you lead is no longer in alignment with your knowledge of your own personal power. Your life is no longer a viable container for your expanding light.

I have been part of the problem, and I have been my own problem. Yet, in my winding, sometimes wayward path, I gained everything I needed to recreate myself and my life as I choose, as can you. Everything has been a gift, even the darkest moments, the turnoffs in the path that led to thorny bushes and brambles that led to seeming dead ends, all of it, because it all is meant to bring you right here, to the point of transformation.

This is the thing: You cannot stand up as the same person who fell down. When you get knocked down, you don't truly fix the situation until you fix yourself. So sometimes, we have to become broken enough that we cannot continue to hobble along, because we're not here to hobble along.

Here is an interesting thing about supermassive black holes like the one at the center of our galaxy. They are usually one part of a binary system, meaning a star and black hole often orbit one another, locked in a dance through the cosmos. When the black hole does not eat its star twin, something amazing happens: a galaxy forms. Thanks to gravity, millions or even trillions of stars gather and begin to orbit the black hole. The bigger the black hole is, the bigger the galaxy that forms around it. Scientists now believe that there is a feedback mechanism that allows growth of both to occur in lockstep.

CHAPTER 1. THE TIME IS NOW

So to recap, consuming matter allows supermassive black holes to grow in size only. It is when such a black hole instead reaches a balance whereby it dances with rather than tries to consume its star twin, that magic happens—that it transforms from a mere black hole to the heart of a galaxy. If it's not yet sufficiently clear, let me reiterate what's been previously said: You already have everything you need to birth something amazing and to recreate yourself as a truer embodied expression of your soul. You are everything you need, and more. You need only look inward.

Feel what you want and who you want to be into existence. This is not about ignoring the ugliness of what is in favor of focusing only on the beauty of what will be. It is a balancing act. When you feel your way through the trauma, programming, and negative emotions, there is a reward on the other side, so meet yourself—all of you—with openness and compassion. You will emerge in a state of gratitude, which in turn brings flow.

I talk about balance a lot because balance fuels manifestation. Balance the time you spend in the outer world and your inner world. Balance what you consume with what you produce. Balance desire with gratitude. It is your nature to create. Balance what you create with what is needed in the world right now. Magic happens when creative passion meets the desire to be of service to the world. Be the universe in service of the universe. This is how we tap into the magic of flow as we become weavers of a better tomorrow.

What this world needs right now more than anything is balance. It is the time for light. Yet darkness, like a child pulling up the covers to ward off the morning, resists. The tug of war intensifies. Evil had a long time to prepare for this war,

RISE: A CALL TO THE LIGHT TRIBE

a long time to grow its tendrils into all facets of this reality. We maintain the equilibrium of the yin yang when we embody the light to the best of our abilities. We have been training for this for lifetimes.

Chapter 2
The Magic of Breaking

For two years, the sound of my old life shattering into a million different pieces was deafening. It's only as the last pieces of an old life fell away that I began to see something more authentic emerging in its place and remembering that I signed up for every situation I have consciously or unconsciously engineered in this life. Things must fall apart so that new ones can come together, just as the seashore would not exist without the destruction of billions of seashells.

Look around you. Things fall apart just to come back together, often simultaneously. It's the nature of the universe, and it's the nature of this planet. So much is crumbling away right now that it's sometimes difficult to comprehend the destruction around us, but as things fall apart that do not serve the planet's evolution, new foundations are being laid for a New Earth. So, why would it not be our nature as well to break as a means of iterative self-actualization?

RISE: A CALL TO THE LIGHT TRIBE

We live in a holographic universe. Our reality is made up of nothing more than information stored on a two-dimensional space, making everything we perceive to be three-dimensional to be nothing more than an illusion. Interestingly, the idea that information is the fifth form of matter is gaining steam in scientific circles, with plans under way to raise money to build a hypersensitive scale that would detect its weight. Like a hologram, the tiniest piece of the whole contains the larger image. As such, a universe is just essentially one enormous room of mirrors, each reflecting towards the other mirrors the entirety of all that is. This is a powerful reminder that what is out there is in here too. Our lives are a reflection of the larger image.

In Hinduism, there is a deity called Akhiandeshvari, which translates roughly into "Never Not Broken." She embodies the power of self-annihilation and re-creation. In life, we are never truly whole. We are born with amnesia. We exist in three-dimensional bodies, disconnected from the many additional dimensions in which our souls concurrently reside. We are repeatedly broken by the world. This is exactly as it should be. It's how we become while simultaneously being. In the black void of our wreckage lies the quiet magic of potential. When nothing is, everything can be. The ash of what has fallen apart is the creative material of the rising phoenix, and she rises even as the flames burn.

Lean into the fall, knowing that it is a necessary lead-in to a new you. Falling into the abyss allows us to finally extend our wings. Allow yourself to feel the breaking into pieces; allow it to inform what is to come. Listen to the stillness left by destruction. This is a magical space; the womb of self-actualization. And the pain? It too is temporary and beautiful.

CHAPTER 2. THE MAGIC OF BREAKING

Perhaps you have seen or heard this, but I'll say it anyway in case you have not. A planted seed knows only that it's been buried. It has no choice but to accept its situation. In its surrender, it breaks open. That is how it blooms. We get figuratively buried so that we too, may bloom. The same occurs with the butterfly. The transformation from caterpillar requires its insides turning into DNA soup so that it may be reformed into a creature of flight. We break so that light can get in. And so that our own light can shine through the cracks. This is transformation. Breathe through it, and into it.

Maybe you can relate. For a long time, I felt a lot like Job from the christian Bible. He was a wealthy man upon whom all manner of hardship and loss was brought as part of a challenge in which God gives Satan permission to torment Job, though he was "blameless" and "upright." Satan claimed that Job served God only because he received God's protection in return, and bets that without such protection, Job would come to curse God. As his children, health and property are taken from him, Job searches for answers, but never condemns God as unjust. He accepts the situation as it is. The recompense for his wisdom was wealth far greater than he lost.

The moral of the story, for those unfamiliar with it, is that we must trust source, even when it appears we are being unfairly smote, because our position is such that we are unable to see the bigger picture or grand design. We do not have to believe in a god in a traditional sense to understand the applicability of this; we live in a friendly universe, and it is always conspiring on our behalf.

A full bowl cannot receive. The new will simply flow right off the top. The bowl must be upended, so that the old no longer occupies space, and new and better things can be received. The upending need not be seen as a crisis—a loss of what was there. Rather, it is an opportunity to make space for better.

We must have the courage to re-imagine ourselves and our lives, bringing matter into greater alignment with spirit each time we break. This is easier said than done, for sure. From rock bottom, the climb back up may sometimes seem daunting, if not impossible. When you have to collect the pieces of yourself as well as your life, things may seem hopeless. But regardless how it may appear from a place of separation and brokenness, you are not alone, You are supremely supported and loved. We are in this together. I see you trying, I thank you, and I breathe with you.

You will rebuild because you must, not only for yourself, but for everyone else here doing the same thing in the name of raising our collective vibration. And trust me, you want to rebuild. This is the incarnation you've been waiting for. We are on an accelerated ascension timeline.

In Hinduism and Buddhism, "nirvana" is an enlightened spiritual state in which souls that have resolved all past karma and learned all needed lessons are released from the endless cycle of samsara—or birth, death, and rebirth—to attain endless bliss. Through the multi-layered process of ascension, we can awaken to our divine nature, shed the parts of our old self that are not well aligned with our inner light, resolve all past karma through the integration of integral lessons, and raise our own and the collective frequency.

The question for you is: How will you rebuild yourself and your life in a way that supports your ascension? Re-imagine yourself and your life as you see fit. Your thoughts are the DNA of your reality.

CHAPTER 2. THE MAGIC OF BREAKING

Consider the zillion different things that had to happen just so for you to come into this material existence, at just this time, and the additional zillions of things, both big and small, that brought you to this step in your journey. You are a miracle manifesting miracles amidst an endless sea of likewise miraculous beings manifesting their own miracles. I think we sometimes forget this, but learning to see the ordinarity of miracles clears the way for more miracles to manifest in our lives.

Let's get back to the analogy of the caterpillar and the butterfly for a moment. As the caterpillar's insides turn to literal goo during its transformation into a butterfly, its cells must organize in new ways. Otherwise, you have nothing more than cells in a cocoon. If we are the cells of a New Earth, we must all imagine ourselves as part of the glorious whole being created, and we must act accordingly.

What remains is what is supposed to remain. However little that may seem, rest assured, it's exactly enough. Own your personal alchemy. Despite appearances, nothing is fixed; everything is possible.

Nassim Haramein, a self-described rebel quantum physicist, explains in a mind-expanding documentary called, "Black Whole: Scientific Evidence that Everything is One," his groundbreaking theory, which elegantly bridges the scholarly chasm between classical physics—the study of the very big expanding out into infinity—and quantum physics—the study of the very small dividing inwards into infinity.

What can appear to take up a finite amount of space, like you, is actually a container for an infinite amount of information. How can this be? We are made of cells, which are made of atoms, which are made of subatomic particles that can be divided into ever-smaller units into infinity. Each time scientists gain the ability to look for something smaller, they find it, Haramein points out. Larger particle accelerators are now able to spot units of energy that are billions of times smaller than the atom.

Likewise, the vacuum is infinitely dense and; what appears to be empty space all around us is anything but empty. It only appears that way because, as Haramein explains, "the geometry of space is so perfectly balanced and polarized in every way possible that it forms what (American Architect, Theorist and Futurist) Buckminster Fuller called a 'vector equilibrium.'"

In other words, you are an infinite universe existing within an infinite universe. And we live fully as the vacuum half the time, as the subatomic particles of which we're made are constantly appearing and disappearing into the quantum field at the speed of light. The double-torus shape and spin of our energy bodies makes this exchange possible, and it's what makes us self-aware, with experiences and understandings that are discrete from everyone else's while simultaneously informing the experiences and understandings of the all.

In simpler terms, what we carry into the void informs it and what we bring back from it informs our material existence—everything from who we are to how we walk in this world to what we have. The intelligent void responds to the information we feed into it. What I am telling you is that things that previously may have seemed impossible are actually very possible for each and every one of us. Every situation with which life presents us is alchemical material, every last thing. This is alchemy of the highest order, but alchemy for which we have been equipped.

So, just how do we alchemize from the things that hurt us, the things that outright undo us? Practice forgiveness

CHAPTER 2. THE MAGIC OF BREAKING

and loving without conditions. When people hurt us, it's often because they are hurting even more. That doesn't mean tolerating bad behavior or compromising your self-respect. But it doesn't have to mean giving up on people either—only on toxic relationship and situational dynamics. Boundaries are a form of balance. Author and clinical psychologist Russell Barkley said that "the children who need love the most will always ask for it in the most unloving ways." This holds true for adults as well. Forgiveness and unflinching love strengthen the grid through which the collective consciousness rises, and facilitates conscious manifestation.

Those with whom we surround ourselves are often our mirrors. To recognize the unhealed darkness in others as healed portions of ourselves is to show compassion for both of us and them. Can you say that you have never been untruthful, never toxic, never jealous, in any lifetime? We all get lost, in various ways and to varying degrees. May how we respond to others' behavior reflect not the pain we feel as the result of their actions, but rather the space we would have liked someone to hold for our healing should we have wandered down that particular path.

You and I are source energy, powerful and self-determining. When we operate from this central fact, we can access our divine power with ease. How do you imagine source energy to be? Forgiveness is a central theme of every world religion and spiritual practice for a reason. Your grief is not without purpose. Personally, I'm grateful for the space to rebuild a life more in alignment with my sense of purpose and self. Things have to fall apart in exactly the way they do to come together better.

We are programmed to chase the career and the house and the spouse and everything else society tells us we need, and many of us spend our entire lives doing that. Sometimes, there are important lessons in the chase; all paths are paths, after all. But what are we ignoring because we're too busy being who and what society says we should be? What is our programming distracting us from?

If you're really lucky, maybe you get to a point on your own when you have the time and energy to finally take stock, to look with curious honesty at your life; to ask how you go there, and if you are who and where you intended to be. Righting that ship can be a formidable task when you've devoted so much time and energy to becoming who you are and getting where you are. It means willingly leaving behind the known for the unknown. Do it on your own or the universe will push you to it.

Marriages break. Loved ones die. Careers disappear. Illness and injury befall us. Pain finds us all. However it happens, we break, maybe partly, maybe fully. But we break, to the extent that we need to, because the universe needs us to step back into ourselves and rebuild ourselves in a way that honors our souls' raison d'etre. And I know that's a big statement within a statement, yet I propose that we all have a reason for being here; it's just that the concept of life's purpose is often misunderstood. We don't have to feel ourselves destined for any one path to have a purpose. For so many of us, purpose begins and ends at expressing the truest version of our souls upon this plane; in other words, shining our light as only we can.

There is often—maybe always—someone or something to blame for the break; the wayward spouse, the abusive parent, the backstabbing boss, the negligent doctor. Rather than blame, forgive the situations and things that were merely playing their roles in service of your remembrance. It may be difficult to see

CHAPTER 2. THE MAGIC OF BREAKING

that through grief, anger, and all the emotions that come along with breaking apart, but trust me, your higher self understands everything to be a gift.

Every day is an opportunity to choose how you grow—through kensho or satori, pain or insight. You have a choice to be proactive or allow the universe to break what it will how it will. Take a sledgehammer to what doesn't serve your purpose here on Earth. It will break anyway. Do not fear what will remain. You may not recognize your life at the end of your process of reconnecting with your purpose, but you will recognize yourself more than ever. It is in the darkness that we can best see our own light. You will see yourself as you were before you came into this lifetime, and you will know exactly what it is you're here to do.

This is what remains at the end of the destruction: a beautifully blank canvas, ready to receive our masterpiece. You are the artist and the artwork. As miracles, manifesting miracles is perfectly natural to us. This understanding is akin to putting on our shoes as we ready for the great journey. Surrender and the path will open before you.

Chapter 3
Walking the Cobbled Road

*N*ew Earth is an ascended Gaia—a super-organism that exists in a higher dimension operating at a higher frequency. It is a new beginning for all, and a new way of being. And it requires us stepping consciously and fully into our creator roles. Regardless of what we are individually creating, what we are co-creating is the rising tide that will carry Gaia and all of its creatures into a new age.

The road to ascension is cobbled. Cobbled in gratitude. In love. In forgiveness. In trust. In resilience. We must embrace and embody each of these divine traits, as they are the cobblestones on the road leading us up. In doing so, we show others what it looks like to walk in light, and awaken others to their divine nature and calling.

See yourself as connected to and supported by source, and express gratitude for all of the good in your life, even if the only good today is breath. Being in a state of gratitude ushers in more

CHAPTER 3. WALKING THE COBBLED ROAD

for which to be grateful. It's the difference between falling and flying. Remember, you chose to be tested in this way. Lose in grace, knowing that an empty vessel can receive more than a full one; and that you are ultimately supported, even when the abyss may seem never-ending. I am grateful for all the goodness that my bowl can now hold.

The universe recognizes as real that to which you give mental energy. If you give lack your mental energy, you will experience more of it. Rather, see all of the ways in which abundance and opportunity appear in your life. See the upended bowl ready to receive new gifts. Act as if what you want is already yours, because it is. You may not yet be connected to that timeline, but you quantum leap by putting yourself in the vibration of what you want to experience. So experience gratitude. Choose the lens through which you view your experiences with care as you think, feel, and speak your world into being.

Before I even get out of bed, I like to start each day by meditating on everything for which I am grateful, starting from that which is nearest, and most essential and expanding outwards as much as I can. This exercise may look a bit different for you, but here is what it looks like for me:

> I have breath. My senses serve me well. I am well. I have a bed and bed sheets under me. A roof covers my head. I get to take a hot shower when I get up. I have tea and a way to make it hot. There is food in my kitchen. I have a kitchen! I have food to feed my animals and myself. I am thankful for every animal and human guide who has ever crossed my path, and though many are no longer with me in body, I am thankful that they remain by my side. I have multiple means of making money,

without having to go into an office. I have a companion who helps me pay my bills, takes care of me when I'm not feeling well, and makes me laugh. I have friends and family who love me and check in on me. I live in a beautiful place with warm winters, and in a country with relative freedom compared to many others. I have a beautiful vision for my future, and the tools to make it my reality. I am so thankful for all the good in my life.

How blessed am I—for who I am and what I know and what I have? How amazingly fortunate am I—for the life I'm creating and who I'm becoming in that process, and for all of the wonder and abundance yet to come? Thank you. Thank you. Thank you.

Gratitude is a doorway to the highest form of love, because when we learn to see everything and everyone as a gift, we learn to love them regardless of the ease of difficulty they bring. All is for your greatest good, so when presented with the choice to retreat into fear or expand into a space of love, choose the latter. Love from a place of unity, knowing that as you heal, the collective of which you are a part heals too. You are a being of love. Act like it. We have been conditioned to let the head lead, yet it is when we allow our hearts to lead us that real magic happens, as love is the only force so powerful that it can transcend death.

Love must start with self. This is not the disfigured love of narcissism, but the love that comes from recognizing our divinity, which is equal to that of all of our brothers and sisters. We are fractals of the great all that is and through which all is possible. How can you not love yourself, truly, when you see what you really are? Yet, love is not just a feeling, is it? Love is a state of being.

CHAPTER 3. WALKING THE COBBLED ROAD

Tell yourself—and your cells—how much you love yourself. Write a reminder on your bathroom mirror, if you must, as I have. "I am enough. I am worthy. I am loved." Your body is a small universe inhabited by countless living organisms. What kind of environment will you create for them? One in which they will thrive, supporting your health and wellbeing, or one in which disease may breed?

When we direct our love inwards, love manifests itself in every aspect of how we treat ourselves. We learn to look in the mirror, to see our flaws without judgment, but rather with compassion for our humanness. We embrace authenticity, for we are just light fragmented into colors of the rainbow—the universe experiencing one of its countless facets. We seek self-accountability as a way to become more like that from which we come. This kind of love is like gravity, pulling us ever in the direction of source.

We are often our own worst enemies, telling ourselves that we are not good enough, that we are not smart enough, that we are not worthy. When we love those voices silent, the natural result is love for our other selves walking alongside us in this world. We begin to see people as we are, and as they are—beautifully flawed, doing their best in a world that doesn't always make much sense. Love facilitates understanding, and understanding breeds more love. It is this love for all who with whom we share this planet that will make New Earth possible.

Maybe you grew up reading the Bible, as I did. Though I do not consider myself a follower of any religion, some gems from the Bible have stayed with me. One of those states: "Love is patient. Love is kind. It does not envy, it does not boast, it is not proud. It is not rude, it is not self-seeking, it is not easily angered, it keeps no record of wrongs. Love does not delight in evil but rejoices in truth." Buddhism, meanwhile, suggests that you "love the whole world as a mother loves her only child." Both speak to a love that is unconditional.

These bodies, this life, this world all impose myriad conditions. Unconditional love brings us into alignment with the essence of who we are—our spirit. This is what ascension is about: becoming the embodiment of spirit.

Loving others unconditionally, just as they are, is easier when we first learn to love ourselves in that way. The ouroboros, the snake eating its own head, is an image interpreted in various ways across cultures and spiritual traditions. Viewed as a symbol of non-duality and infinite renewal—as the one soul—it is a lot like the light of love. Buddha said it well: "If you light a lamp for somebody, it will also brighten your path." Love for others ultimately feeds you, for you and they are all the same.

People and situations will hurt us because they must to help us grow into clearer alignment with our highest selves, and to help us live our stories. This is what it means to live in Christ consciousness. Even as he was being taken to be crucified, Jesus said, "Father, forgive them, for they do not know what they are doing."

For one, every last one of us is doing our best to get through this life, sometimes with limited means, such as knowledge and empathy. So recognize that the ignorance, hatefulness, greed, or whatever else we may judge in others, is simply those others or those selves operating to the best of their abilities with whatever biology, programming, and circumstances are at their disposal. We are swords forged from the same metal sharpening each other. Thus, forgive until there is nothing to forgive because you understand that all is part of a grand design. The bad things that happen to us, often at the hands of others, are bad because we

CHAPTER 3. WALKING THE COBBLED ROAD

judge them to be that way, thus setting ourselves up for suffering. A more useful perspective is that everything happens for our divine evolution, and sometimes it happens as a result of others' confusion as they stumble around in this grand illusion.

Second, Jesus had to die on the cross to show us the reality of ascension and to demonstrate Christ consciousness so that we may embody it, for we are in a way the second coming—each and every one of us stepping into Christ consciousness, donning the rainbow light body of Buddhism, to create heaven on earth. Everything that has happened had to happen to get us here and to catapult us into what is to come.

This story has already been written from beginning to beginning, as time is not linear, but more like the fabric of space, stretching in every direction from every direction. As actors in one of the many threads or timelines that make up the fabric of this space-time, we are not privy to the whole story, but only to the pieces that unfold before us in linear manner, just as the singular microbe in our gut can't have any idea as to what the whole of us looks like. Our job, like the microbe, is to play out our roles to the best of our abilities in support of that greater one that we can merely begin to sense.

Knowing this, how can we not forgive what had to happen to each of us for us to become the wayshowers to New Earth? We are the ones we've been waiting for, but we're not the only ones who've been waiting for us. And we are here now, ready to forge ahead, so forgive everyone and everything, for they are you and you them, each of us chiseling away at each other to sculpt a masterpiece.

Forgiveness is a catalyst of healing. Yet, it's one thing to say you should forgive, and another entirely to actually forgive, isn't it? Forgiveness can be difficult; I get it. We are taught that we should forgive. We are taught to say the words. Yet, we are not often taught how to forgive. For me, forgiveness is a lot like a recipe. Different ingredients go into forgiveness, like empathy for those who wrong us, seeing the gift in the painful, and gratitude for lessons learned. And the more we use the recipe, the better the dish comes out.

But before we even begin cooking, we have to prepare the space. This is done by creating detachment from any alternate storyline, from any "if only," scenario and from the trap of deluding ourselves to protect our egos. What happened happened as it did, and as it was meant to. Thus, we find ourselves in position to begin cooking, and "I was abused" or "I was betrayed," can become "I am a survivor" or "I am strong." We then begin to see those who hurt us as other versions of us playing other parts in a script to provide us with an experience we needed to step into our current selves.

Several years ago, I stumbled onto an excellent guided visualization forgiveness exercise by a company called Mindvalley that integrates what I see as all of the ingredients of forgiveness into a beautiful formula. It's an exercise based on the research of the Biocybernaut Institute into forgiveness and its effects on the brain. I've adapted it to fit what works for me and those with whom I work to facilitate healing.

To start, choose one person, situation, or thing in your life that you wish to forgive. If there is no name or face, visualize the feeling the situation or thing brings up in you. For instance, a looming shadow or big, angry squiggle—whatever works for you. When we can assign an antagonist role to a person, forgiveness is more straightforward than when we are unable to do that. For instance, with unremembered childhood abuse and certain types

CHAPTER 3. WALKING THE COBBLED ROAD

of sexual trauma, you may feel violated, you may have an inner knowing of the trauma without being able to recall specifics, like who did it. For this exercise, it doesn't matter, because forgiveness is really for you, not for them.

You see, what is unforgiven creates a strong negative charge in our lives. This charge is a lot like a downed tree on the cobbled path. You may think that you can sidestep it and continue onwards, but the negative charge continues to impact you in unseen ways. It is a block, preventing the good flowing down from reaching us. To counter the negative charge of the unforgiven, we must create an equally strong positive charge. True forgiveness does that for us.

Remember, forgiveness isn't just for people. It's also for the situations we have put or found ourselves in, or the things in life that have caused us suffering. An experience of lack, for instance, may benefit from forgiveness. While that may seem silly, what we're really doing is removing the negative charge these things have over us, because when we do that, the situations tend to be less persistent.

You may need to do this exercise more than once, and maybe many times. Forgiveness is a practice. It's not a one and done thing. The great thing about this exercise is that it helps you determine when you are done—when you're really clear or the emotional charge associated with the person, situation, or thing you wish to forgive.

At certain points, you may feel uncomfortable, sad, and angry. That's okay. Feel your feelings. Maybe you've heard that saying, "the only way is through." What we're doing here is the through. Remember that you are safe. Let's begin:

Start by closing your eyes. Breathe in slowly and deeply through your nose, in for a four count if that feels comfortable. Exhale through your mouth, again for a four count. Continue doing this, focusing on your breath. As you exhale, feel any tension you may have, and anything that doesn't serve you, leaving your body. We can learn so much from trees. Let's practice being like them for a bit. Feel your legs sinking deep into the soil beneath you like roots reaching down into the core of Gaia. Feel the nutrients of the rich soil nourishing you from the bottom up. Straighten your spine, as your branches reach up to the sky, basking in the moonlight. You are a pillar of light, pure consciousness connected to both earth and sky.

Now, bring your awareness to your heart. Feel light pouring out from your heart and creating a protective bubble around you. Maybe this bubble expands a little each time you breathe. Let it expand until you feel completely protected within it.

Visualize yourself standing in a place that is relevant to the person, situation, or thing that you wish to forgive. It might be a childhood home, for instance. Look around you. It is just you here right now. But you won't be alone for long.

It's time to assemble a council of trusted advisors. Take a couple of minutes to think of three beings whose integrity and counsel you trust. These may be people you know or have known, or perhaps your pets (present or past), or even someone you've never met but who you want in your corner as a trusted advisor. They can be anyone, and they don't have to be living, as we're simply calling on their energy. Visualize these

CHAPTER 3. WALKING THE COBBLED ROAD

three beings standing behind you. They are here to support you.

Now visualize the person, situation, or thing that you wish to forgive in front of you, maybe six feet away. Take a few minutes to tell this person or thing in front of you exactly what they did to you, and how that made you feel. If you feel the need to yell at them, imagine yourself doing so. Get it all out. Keep your eyes closed, and remember, you are safe and protected within your bubble of light.

Once you have finished expressing your feelings, visualize the person or thing growing in reverse in front of you, until they are a small child, of no more than five or six years of age. Take a good look at this small child before you. What does it look like? Is it scared? Angry? Hurt? Consider what may have happened to this child to make it into the adult or big scary thing that hurt you. Is there a chance what you experienced was a reflection of something in them—something that hurt them the same way?

Consider how your life has been positively impacted by however they hurt you. What's the silver lining? If nothing else, it brought you here, to a place of learning to forgive so that you may become a forgiving person. What other positives have come out of it? Sometimes they're difficult to see, but life always brings us good with the bad.

When you are ready, tell this child you forgive them, and ask for their forgiveness in return if you feel it is needed, then visualize yourself hugging this small child. How do they feel in your arms? How do you feel? Remember, it is just a child. They didn't know any better.

RISE: A CALL TO THE LIGHT TRIBE

They didn't understand they were just passing on the hurt someone inflicted on them.

Once you are finished hugging them, step back and call on your counsel of three. Ask each advisor, one at a time, if you're done here. Be still. You may see a nod or hear a quiet "yes." Or perhaps you'll get a "no," or a shake of the head. Only when each member of your council gives you a clear "yes" have you completely cleared the negative charge from this situation. You don't have to repeat the exercise now, but you should do so when you're ready to give it a second go if you got even one "no." Your council's response tells you how far you have to go—how many layers this onion has.

Once you've gotten a response from each council member, you may visualize the person or thing and place of dissolving in front of you. Focus again on your breathing, noticing that you are still encased in a bubble of light emanating from your heart. Breathe deeply, in through the nose and out through your mouth, releasing all that doesn't serve you on the exhale, and opening your eyes when you feel ready.

When we learn to forgive others, we are well on our way. Yet, forgiveness is a two-way street. We may unknowingly be the bad guy in someone else's story. Each of us sees the world in our own way, and our truth is valid for us. Yet, their truth is truth too. Quantum physics is now catching up to the fact that we are all living in our own versions of the universe. Our reality is affected by our view of it. So it's likely that at some point, though you may see yourself blameless in your interactions with friends, family members, and acquaintances, someone has been hurt by your words or actions.

CHAPTER 3. WALKING THE COBBLED ROAD

We also cause harm by merely living, by our use of natural resources, and in the consumption of things that rely on unethical production practices and the modern equivalent of slave labor. Often, we just don't know; after all, so much of our world is constructed so that the things we pick off shelves in stores are completely disconnected from the stories of how they came to be produced. Yet, if we saw the small, impoverished child slaving away barefoot in a dangerous mine for the components of our many inexpensive electronics—if we could see him as another aspect of ourselves in suffering—we might feel called to action.

The child in the mine is a difficult problem to solve, despite our determination to right that wrong. Tracking down the small, fly-by-night operations in third-world countries that supply those who supply the producers of our electronics with the necessary minerals may simply be a problem bigger than us. Asking for forgiveness is sometimes the only recourse we have. And yet, sometimes we might not even know from whom we must ask it.

I cannot stress the power of ho'oponopono, an ancient Hawaiian balancing prayer. It consists of the following four phrases, said one after the other: "I am sorry. Please forgive me. Thank you. I love you."

Say it to yourself. Say it to others, whether they can hear you or not. Say it to the unified field that connects everything and everyone. Say it to the parts of your body that have failed you or are failing you. Say it to the trees. Say it daily, because by our mere existence, we create situations requiring forgiveness. But maybe most of all, say it to the water, that living, liquid being that makes all life possible.

RISE: A CALL TO THE LIGHT TRIBE

Science has shown that the structural makeup of water allows water molecules to hold memories. Our water remembers all through which it has passed, and all that has passed through it. Our bodies are mostly water. When we take in water, we take in the memories of those molecules of water we ingest. Never mind that we pollute our drinking supply with fluoride and our natural waterways with countless chemicals and trash.

Consider too that our water system is a closed-loop system made up of pipes in all kinds of L-shaped formations. Water is meant to flow naturally, circularly. But in this man-made system, each time water reaches a turn in the pipes, it experiences the trauma of a sudden stop and forced redirection. Flow is suddenly halted and redirected. We shower with this water. We drink this water. Water is a superconductor of our intentions, yet our water reaches us and leaves us wounded. When we are wounded, we do not function as well. The same goes for our water. Ho'oponopono is a tool for remediating this problem. And because we are part of the great web of life, healing water helps to heals us.

Trust, the fourth cobblestone on the road to New Earth, is a lot like magic pixie dust, or the Aramaic "avra kehdabra," from which "abracadabra" comes, meaning, "I will create as I speak." Trust imprints our intentions into the unified field, fueling their manifestation.

Trust above all, that what is happening is happening for you rather than to you. Learn to float. Allow the universe to hold you up, rather than fighting it because you do not understand it. When we fight the tides, we drown. Acceptance for your journey can be difficult when you can't see where the path is taking you. You may ask, "Why me?" I will tell you why. You are

CHAPTER 3. WALKING THE COBBLED ROAD

so important to this planet's evolution that spirit is taking every necessary measure to ensure you are on task. It is simply time to level up. Trust that.

Trust hasn't always been easy for me, and maybe it hasn't been for you either. People will always let us down. What I've learned to trust is that when someone lets me down, it's because there is something for me to learn in the disappointment. Discernment is important here. The fact that people have let us down does not mean that we should not trust. Trust yourself, even when it seems you are your own worst enemy, for we all engineer the situations and conditions we need for growth.

Most of all, trust spirit. It is our most basic spiritual building block. The marriage of spirit to matter (our bodies) births the soul upon first breath. This is a belief taught by ancient spiritual traditions through the tree of life sacred geometry, and it is knowledge that resonates deeply within me personally. Souls are closest to spirit when we are born, not yet conditioned by the world, subject only to the limits of our biology. Soul is what we are under our beliefs, programming, conditioning, roles, and perspectives. It's what we find when we leave the chatter of the mind behind. Spirit is the oneness waiting when we go even deeper. The no one and all one, in no time and all time. Spirit is truth.

When you hear the universe calling you in one direction or another, go unafraid. When we trust in the realness of what spirit communicates to us and act accordingly, we are fully supported by the universe. And why would we not be—we are here on its behalf, to help in this great planetary shift. So trust too that the tools needed to do what is for you to do are at your disposal.

Chapter 4
Spiraling Upwards

Though it may appear otherwise when we look from within the matrix, we are each responsible for every last thing we experience—perhaps not we the humans, but certainly we as souls. This life is a crash course in manifesting. When we ask, we receive, just not always how we expect, and sometimes we must be willing to lose to make space for what is to come.

I am in the process of remaking my reality as I remake myself. I told the universe the kind of person I wanted to be—kind, brave, and free, and it set into motion a series of events by which I could return to being all of those things. I say return rather than grow because I know I have those things in me, as do you.

We are perfect beings of light having limiting human experiences, but through human experiences we can remember our true nature. Sometimes we get tied up in how we think things should be or happen, but the universe isn't concerned with such details. As a result, we fail to see that what we are experiencing

CHAPTER 4. SPIRALING UPWARDS

is part of a process designed to achieve an outcome we have asked for, consciously or unconsciously. We chose to come into this human existence, and we chose the lessons we need to learn to manifest the selves needed to achieve what we came here for. What are you choosing now?

In writing this, I magnify my manifestation abilities. Herein lies the alchemy. Belief precedes creation. Matter is birthed by thoughts. Align yourself with the vibration of what you want, and the universe will rearrange itself to make that so.

We are all multi-dimensional beings, existing simultaneously in many parallel dimensions and many concurrent yet differing timelines. Somewhere, the intentions you set for yourself on this plane of existence have already come to pass elsewhere. It's how the collective unconscious evolves—by giving us the opportunity to try out—and learn from—every possible scenario we can imagine for ourselves.

Somewhere in this multidimensional universe, there is a version of you for whom the wishes you hold in this time and space have already come to pass. What you desire is already yours. You've just not caught up to that timeline. But just how does one connect to a timeline that exists concurrently in another dimension? By tapping into the vibration of that existence to integrate that experience into this reality. Feel what you want as yours, and it will be.

In scientific terms, we're talking about the principle of quantum entanglement, which states that everything that has once been connected is always intrinsically connected, and what affects one particle affects the others in real-time. All the pieces of your soul across the fabrics of time and space remain connected. You just may not see it, simply because of the illusory nature of our existence as human beings. But across time and space, what you want is already yours.

Know that it is yours, feel it as yours, and it—whatever that may be—will materialize in this plane. Interesting, quantum physics is just catching up to the fact that thoughts and emotions do indeed influence matter. There is no need to wish it into existence, because it already is.

That is what seeing the matrix can do for us—allow you to be better captains of our ships. So ask for what you need to live a meaningful, heart-led life, so that you can shine as the beacon of light you are. Ask, for you shall receive. Maybe not on the timeline of your choice, and maybe not as you imagine, but receive you shall. Understand that there may be a cost to what you ask for, and that the universe will require you to show up and accept the challenges before you just as it is showing up for you by weaving magic on your behalf.

We create ourselves and our lives, but we do so much more than that. Each one of us is a fractal of the divine source from which we come and to which we return; perfect, luminous beings both freed and limited by our bodies, having human experiences colored by circumstances, experiences, and bodily architecture and chemistry, but ultimately here to be expressions of spirit, to evolve through experience, and thus feed into the greater evolution of all that is. Trust the process and let come what may, with gratitude for what your journey will teach you and where it will lead, and with forgiveness and love for every other being on this planet with you.

Are you ready to manifest a new you in service of a New Earth? We are spiraling upwards. I'm not saying it won't be a rough ride up, but take heart. Many of us walk this path with you.

CHAPTER 4. SPIRALING UPWARDS

We are your team and you ours. Search for us as we seek you out, so that we may support one another through this process. This is the great shift, and it begins with you.

Part 2
Transcendence in A Broken World

Chapter 5
The Fear Trap

Fear is such a powerful emotion, but the power it yields over us is perhaps the most harmful thing there is. Yet every aspect of our lives is bookended by fear. We must go to work and make money, or we may find ourselves homeless. We abide by the rules of whatever religion we choose to follow, lest we face punishment in the afterlife. There is something to fear everywhere we look, and it seems that list grows by the day, making fear an undercurrent running through all of society.

The thing about fear is that more often than not, it's a trap. Why waste time and energy feeling anxious and worrying about things that may never come to pass? Of course, it's one thing to say that, and another completely to live it, because as humans, we are conditioned to fear. At one time, this evolutionary trait helped us avoid being eaten by lions and tigers or killed by warring tribes. Fearing the right things kept our ancestors alive. It's a different world today, and our fears tend to be more about a lack of understanding or control than actual survival. Statistically speaking, car rides are far more dangerous than flying, but fear of flying is more common. It's the same case with sharks. Fewer people die from shark attacks than from being struck by falling coconuts, but more people fear shark attacks than falling coconuts.

While some fears are justifiable, all of society is structured to keep us in fear. Why? Think of the false matrix—the invisible programming and insidious systems that keep us living as hamsters on wheels unaware of our divinity and oneness—like code on a computer. Fear is the electricity that allows the code to operate. Fear is a constricting emotion. It is dense. It weighs us down to this third-dimensional reality.

Being fully present in the now is the way up, how we evolve into our best potential. Yet, when we fear something, we are not living in the present moment. We are stuck in a potential future, a potential that may or may not happen. And in fact, the anxiety—or persistent worry about a fear—can create a self-fulfilling prophecy. Our thoughts shape our reality. The universe doesn't know the difference between a fear and a hope; it sees only what we give mental energy to, and uses that as creative direction.

Thus, our fears may cause what we fear to come true, leaving us with a past basis for fearing the thing in the future. In other words, the world is scary because it has proven itself to be so in the past, and so we become scared of what it may bring in the future. Once we get swept into the undercurrent, it just keeps pulling us further from center in a vicious cycle. Do you see the trap now?

Likewise, consider what we do to our bodies when you spend time in fear. Science has shown that living in fear can lead to

CHAPTER 5. THE FEAR TRAP

everything from a weakened immune system to gastrointestinal and cardiovascular damage. It can speed up aging and death. It's not what we fear that is killing us; it's the fear itself. Fear places us in a fight-or-flight state, triggering a chain of reactions that starts in our brains and affects our entire bodies. Being in a chronic state of fear can impair memory and damage certain parts of the brain that allow us to regulate emotions and make rational decisions. Over time, it can become even more challenging to regulate fear, leading to chronic anxiety and fatigue, clinical depression, and even post-traumatic stress disorder.

Remember, your body is a universe for all of your cells and selves. Fear creates an ideal environment for disease to thrive. And, as within, so without. Fear is a contagious frequency.

There has not been so much fear in recent history as there is now. People everywhere are dying in record numbers from COVID-19 even while some who are eligible to receive vaccines reject them. Many in the United States and elsewhere are polarizing towards the political end of the spectrum that led to Adolf Hitler's Germany. Late-stage capitalism and all of the societal ailments caused by a consumption-driven society are simultaneously ravaging us and Mother Earth, with frightening symptoms that include homelessness, hunger, and disease staring us now everywhere in the face. With hate crimes on the rise, we're seeing hatred that has long been hidden rising to the surface. Diving lines grow deeper as otherness insinuates itself further into the unconscious collective. The black hole appears to be leading the dance with its star twin.

Yes, it can be difficult to not be afraid in such a climate. Yet, fear is the least helpful emotion in this situation. With a weakened immune system from the body's fear response, we can become more susceptible to that which would consume us. Thoughts create reality. Remember, the universe doesn't know the difference between what we want or don't want. It simply knows that we're giving something space in our heads, and takes that as material from which to create your reality. Curate your thoughts carefully.

As gods of our inner universes and co-creators of our shared reality, the environment we create is entirely up to us. So how can we choose not to live in fear? After all, our bodies are still wired to react to fear, even if the fight or flight response is useless against our modern fears, like whether we'll be able to continue paying our bills or if the world is about to end at the hands of humans.

Given that fear begins in our brains, the antidote to fear must begin in our hearts. As with every other feeling, the way out of fear is through. Allow yourself to bear witness to your fear, observing what it does to your body and how it makes you feel, without getting caught up in it. Think of it like dark, passing clouds. You are the sky. Allow the fear to be, yet recognize that it is not you, simply something you are experiencing.

Send love outwards as you send love inwards, and you may find your fear softening. Bring your awareness to your heart space, allowing yourself to be enveloped in a bubble of love emanating from within you. Just as forgiveness neutralizes anger, love is the emotional charge that can neutralize fear.

Thank your body for doing its best to keep you safe while simultaneously asking yourself why you feel that fear. Sometimes, as is the case with phobias, there is no logical reason beyond our programming. Fear is often a learned behavior. As a child, I learned to be afraid of insects from watching adults' overreaction

CHAPTER 5. THE FEAR TRAP

to them. Where do your phobias come from? Can you look back in time at the points when you acquired them? Replay the scenario, so that you may see the irrationality of the reactions of those who inadvertently taught you to be afraid, and send them love too. In this way, we can energetically re-parent others, fostering understanding rather than fear.

If we dig deep, we may find lack of understanding at the core of our fears. But remember, we are all spirit. We are all individuations of the one. This is even true with insects. We are so much more alike than we may realize. The roach is constantly reacting to stimulus, seeking what it needs to survive while fleeing that which might bring harm, like the bottom of a shoe. Aren't we all doing just that—trying to survive while avoiding harm? Reacting to the best of our abilities to whatever unexpected situations may arise?

Deep, slow breaths can help to bring the body from a fight-or-flight state to rest-and-digest mode, which is the opposite of a trauma response. I like inhaling through the nostrils for an eight count, holding for a four count, and then breathing out slowly for an eight count through the mouth. I also don't wait until I need to bring myself down, but rather practice this breathing for two-minute intervals several times a day. This way, I am always in a better position to respond rationally to whatever may come my way, rather than react from a place of emotional programming.

Acknowledge and thank your mind for trying to keep you safe. It does not know that the fear is hurting you. You may find it useful to visualize your mind as a small child. Send it love, gratitude, and reassurance. And then ask it to relinquish the need to be in control. Let it know that it is your co-pilot, "co" being the operative part of that. Invite it to learn to see past illusion by stepping into an observer role so that it can make more rational, helpful decisions. This is how we alchemize reaction-based living into response-based living, and how we create space in which understanding can flourish.

Reactions happen quickly, typically without much thought. They are a survival-based defense mechanism. Often, the lack of thought that goes into reactions leads us to regret our actions. Using the example of an unwanted bug in our living space, a reaction of fear may lead us to eliminate the fear—by killing the harmless bug, which has as much a right as we do to life. A response, on the other hand, is thought-out and made calmly and makes use of information from both our conscious and subconscious. But both start the same—in this case, with something that triggers fear in us.

Responding involves stepping back time to observe the situation with our rational mind. We may still fear the bug, but we recognize that it is harmless and that we do not really want to kill it (rational conscious mind), because that is not who we are (loving subconscious), so we may devise a different way to remove it from our space.

When it comes to interactions with other humans, reacting can take a bad situation and make it worse, whereas responding allows us to consider the best actions for resolving the situation and returning to a place of understanding and cooperation. The key, again, is being able to step back from the emotion, and bearing witness to it rather than allowing it to animate us like a marionette. Use breath to create this space between you and the emotion.

Ultimately, there is a lot outside of our control that can

CHAPTER 5. THE FEAR TRAP

seem scary. But guess what? You're not the driver. Rather than seeing that as a source of anxiety, I have learned to see it as a source of relief.

I no longer get overwhelmed from trying to control everything in my life, because I have come to understand that the force in control is much more powerful and much more capable than me. It has gotten me to right now in one piece. It has always held me safe. Even when it didn't seem like anyone was driving this car, I always ended up right where I was supposed to be, learning the lessons meant for me and becoming a better version of me.

So let go. You were never really in control anyway. What will come will come. Allow yourself the mental space to be present with your journey, not worrying about the future or attempting to avoid reliving the past. You have a capable driver. Trust this. This trust makes the journey so much more enjoyable. You can look out the window unafraid, jam out to some music even, knowing full well that while there is so much that could go wrong and maybe that is indeed going "wrong," whatever happens is exactly what is meant to happen for your highest good.

Do not judge the experience as right or wrong—it is just what is. You can't see the full picture as the protagonist of your own story; you lack all the information to make such a judgment. What seems like a stroke of bad luck now could later turn out to be a blessing in disguise.

And, you are not losing anything by recognizing that you are not in control. Quite the opposite, so many possibilities open up when you give up control to something greater than yourself. Sometimes, when we pull our grip off the steering wheel of our lives, the result is so much better than we could have ever imagined. Give the universe the opportunity to surprise you, and it very likely will.

What does it look like to live without fear? Some discernment is needed here. Let's use COVID-19 as an example. This virus is real. It can impact anyone, including me, at any time. The prevailing advice for preventing its further spread is to employ social distancing, and when it's necessary to go out, that we wear face masks. I do not fear catching the virus; if I'm meant to catch it, I will regardless of what precautions I take. That doesn't mean I shouldn't take precautions. It's a case of preparing for the worst, but expecting the best. And it's not just for me. Following these recommendations is as much an act of self-love as it is an act of compassion for my fellow human beings. If I can do something that might prevent the suffering and even death of another, why would I not? This is a chance to be who I say I am. This is self-accountability.

Let me propose another reason for engaging in this kind of discernment. Because fear lowers the immune system, increasing the likelihood of illness, and because I do not want to play a role in increasing others' fear levels, I do what I can, not just to prevent the spread of illness, but also to prevent the spread of fear. When people see that we are all in this together, a sense of communal trust and strength can be established that overrides fear.

Because we are so intrinsically interconnected, my actions eventually swing back around to benefit me. You see, for those who are energetically sensitive, fear doesn't have to be ours to be felt. So, if I do my part to reduce fear among my fellow human beings, I am also reducing the level of external fear with which I

CHAPTER 5. THE FEAR TRAP

come into contact as I move about, albeit in limited ways, in the world during this time.

I'm going to take this even further. Let's talk about what Albert Einstein called "spooky action at a distance." At the time, Einstein could not explain the principle of quantum entanglement, but he knew it existed, so he called it "spooky action at a distance."

Since Einstein, quantum physics has proven the existence of quantum entanglement—the concept that what affects one object can affect another that was at some point in time been connected to it, regardless of the present distance between the two objects. What happens to one object as the result of some stimulus can happen to another to which it had previously been somehow connected, immediately, without even a nanosecond of time between their response, as if looking at a mirror. So everything that has at any point in the past been connected is still somehow connected. If you believe in the Big Bang, then you must believe that we were at one point, all connected. Belief systems that include a creator deity also link us as energetic brothers and sisters.

So, if we are all connected, and what affects one physically can equally affect others, given the wildfire-like spread of COVID-19, I am left to wonder if another force, beyond the traditional explanations of person-to-person spread, is responsible for this pandemic. We are living in a time when, as consciousness rises, the veil between us all thins, meaning our interconnectedness has never been this strong.

Some scientists who study quantum entanglement now believe that having a strong bond—perhaps like that created by love—with someone increases entanglement. So what physically affects the particles of those we love may affect ours as well, regardless of physical proximity. If someone we care about is affected by the virus, is there then a chance that we might be as well, even if we have never come into physical contact with it? It's a real possibility.

However, quantum entanglement is a two-way street. So, what if our zen outlook and resulting robust immune system can mean, for someone who is infected, the difference between a few mild symptoms and hospitalization? We can choose to let the world imprint onto us, or we can imprint onto the world.

I get it. It's often difficult, particularly for empaths, to live in today's broken world. It can hurt to look unflinchingly at the suffering around us, particularly when we do not know how we can help or do not have the tools to help. We must not fear looking, for only then can we direct the healing light from our hearts where it is most needed.

We are co-creators of this universe, you and I. But it's up to each of us whether we passively receive the vibration that others emit, or whether we actively exude a vibration of our own out into the world. When enough of us emit the same vibration, we create an energetic hug for those who need it, helping them consciously or subconsciously rise out of the fear vibration to match our own.

In embodying the vibration of light, we serve as guideposts for others who do not yet see their own ability to shine, and who have not yet in this incarnation seen themselves as the infinitely luminous beings they are. This is how we collectively transcend the fear trap and fuel the rise in consciousness. We are so much powerful than we may realize. Just as the dark ones are here so that we may see ourselves in contrast to them, so too are we here to awaken others to their own light.

CHAPTER 5. THE FEAR TRAP

When we step outside of ourselves and look unflinchingly and detachedly at ourselves and our lives, we can gain a better picture of what is. I am. You are. I am because you are. And when we stop giving power to our fears and instead reclaim that power, we transcend brokenness. We are able to move about in the world with purpose as agents of light. This process of transmuting fear is the gold used to put together the broken vase—both which is us and in which we find ourselves.

Chapter 6
Taking Stock

This book has been a long time in the making. Every time I sat to write, the demands of the new life I've been busy building called to me. Yet now there is no choice but to write. You see, something happened. The world changed.

Mother Gaia, in all her wisdom, has made us stand still, if only for a while. While so many suffer from a pandemic, there is reason to rejoice. The world has been burning for a long time now, both figuratively and literally. The Amazon, Africa, and Australia were in flames for months during 2019. Untold numbers of beings perished. California burns seemingly every summer now. Our oceans' creatures have been washing up dead en masse, their corpses filled with plastic pollution. Whales in the South Pacific are dying of starvation, like so many people across the globe, while nations' wealth goes to the war machine. More than any other year, 2020 felt like watching a horror movie play out each day. Yet it never stops. We never stop.

CHAPTER 6. TAKING STOCK

Because it seems that people are okay with suffering when they can watch it at a distance. When it's a family crying after their home has been bombed to ashes in Syria, a starving child in Yemen, or even a shoeless man on the side of the road. Maybe we feel the problems are too distant and too great, so we look away rather than face them.

And so, we have the coronavirus named COVID-19 to thank, for showing us that we are all interconnected, that what harms one harms all, and that the actions of individuals matter. Thank you, Gaia, for bringing the destruction to our doorstep, so that we have no choice but to face the fact that we've done this, and it's ours to fix—all of it.

We're responsible for the deforestation, the plastic in our oceans, the homelessness, and all manner of pestilence. Every time we choose blind consumerism, every time we vote against the environment, and every time we choose to look away rather than figure out how we might help. I hear you, your aunt, the one with the compromised immune system, didn't choose to catch the coronavirus. Your neighbor's husband didn't choose to die from it. But they made countless unconscious choices over the course of their lives—like you and I—that allowed COVID-19 to become the threat it became.

It is thought that the virus may have originated in a bat or pangolin that ended up in a Chinese "wet" market, in which live animals are sold for consumption. Another theory for which there seems to be some evidence is that the virus was created in a lab and tested on an animal that was then sold to a wet market. It is common practice for lab animals to end up in such markets, because researchers in China are poorly paid. Sometimes, these animals are consumed while alive as well. Can you imagine the nightmare they endure? As we continue to encroach into the world's remaining wild spaces, more animals are at risk of human consumerism from the scientific community, the exotic animal trade, trophy hunting, the demand for traditional medicines that use animal parts, and the desire for culinary novelty.

COVID-19 is just the latest karmic debt for our cruelty as a species. And it won't be the last. But at least it provided a much-needed time-out. Will we as a species reconsider our collective actions and move forward in a new, more compassionate direction? Or will we continue onwards like the bully who fails to learn their lesson? Unfortunately, it seems to be the latter.

Some have called this The Great Turning; a time when, collectively brought to our knees, we have no choice but to hold each other in mourning, because regardless of which direction we look in, we see our own grief reflected back. And so we see that the other is really us. In this realization lies the opportunity for rebirth. What a beautifully hopeful perspective.

A prophecy that has been attributed to the Hopi, Cree, and even to an evangelical religious tract talks about the time of the rainbow warriors:

> When the earth is ravaged and the animals are dying, a new tribe of people shall come unto the earth from many colors, classes, creeds, and who by their actions and deeds shall make the earth green again. They will be known as the "Warriors of the Rainbow."
>
> The Rainbow Warriors will be strong in their love and powerful in their compassion. They will be imbued with the willpower to save the voiceless ones, the plants and animals, because they understand our earthly

CHAPTER 6. TAKING STOCK

relationship. They will impart the values of life, not death, or relationship, not violence, of pace, not war.

Regardless of origin, the fact remains that seers across time and space have foretold of this time. We the ones foretold to rise from the ashes. But while it's nice to think that we are so close to the beginning, that's perhaps unlikely. This is more likely the very beginning of a long, brutal end. We cannot expect centuries of living as if everything we've taken, everything we've done to this land and to its inhabitants, to be atoned for with this virus. Our karmic debt is much, much higher.

There is hope, for sure. China banned the sale and consumption of wild animals. England decided to house the homeless. Even governments seem to be changing in response to this plague we've brought upon ourselves. The United States turned away, though by an uncomfortably small margin—from the perils of fascism in electing a kinder president. The Brazilian president who turned the other way while the Amazon Rainforest after dismantling environmental protection policies faces investigation by the international criminal court.

More people are beginning to see that ensuring everyone can afford to eat and see a doctor should be universal rights. They are beginning to want for others what they want for themselves. This is a choice point. So many systems must collapse for a better world to emerge. There will be resistance. There will be suffering. Still, we must collectively choose to lean into the break. May we allow all that hasn't worked for all to shatter into a zillion unrecognizable pieces, so that we may create something better.

The pandemic has been a call to awaken to our purpose. We are here to lead the great procession out of darkness. Our light must be as bright as the darkness is black. We must be brutally honest, both with ourselves and others, about where we are and how we got here. This is a collective looking in the mirror. It requires all of us to do this difficult work. Sticking our heads in the sand just won't do. It's not okay to ignore the "hysterical" media, not enough to just focus on projecting good vibes. We are all responsible for what we're facing now. This is a time to look courageously at our grim reality. To ask how our individual actions or inactions have fueled this collective shit storm, and to ask how we might change our behavior to show others the way out.

We must remain vigilant to our privilege. Traditionally, being white, being male, being able-bodied, being a citizen of a first-world country have afforded so many a kind of blissful blindness. COVID-19 illuminated a different kind of privilege too: people who feel themselves to be immune from the virus, either because of a healthy immune system or because of a belief that they have divine protection, threaten us all. The virus may leave them untouched, but they may come in contact with others whose defenses are not so strong and who could die. We are responsible for one another. And it's not about the virus alone, but the mindset it reveals. We as a society must care about the weakest among us.

Vigilance against privilege is the essence of the Rainbow Warrior. Though we may walk as lions on the savanna, we must take care not to ravage that upon which we come into contact. We must be guardians of all because all is us. This is, after all, a revolution of love, because only love is strong enough to counter all the damage we've done.

As we continue our descent into destructive chaos, it is up to us to ask, "How will I respond?" Were you part of the solution? Or did you stick your head in the sand and resist a breaking of what served us not?

CHAPTER 6. TAKING STOCK

When we face our situation with acceptance, we can take control of our part in the collective response. We can also learn to thread more gently, to walk more kindly alongside every life form with which we share this planet. We can begin to behave in the best interest of all.

Around us, systems in society are crumbling. These are the systems that taught us that we must work endlessly for the right to live comfortably; that we are useless if we are not producing; that money is more important than kindness; and that the ability to eat, learn, and see a doctor should cost us; that when a person steals what they need, they have committed a crime deserving of punishment, but when industry steals its employees time, energy, and wellbeing, it's just doing business and should be rewarded with tax breaks and government subsidies. Let us witness the crumbling of unjust systems as we simultaneously look within us to those parts of us that have bought into those systems and false programming. Let us emerge from our time of reflection ready to birth the new.

There's no going back. There is nothing there but what led us here. Burn in the fire of transformation, so that you may rise up with love, courage, and compassion. You are here to lead others out from the flames, and it must start now. New Earth must begin to emerge even as the old one burns.

This is staking stock—looking around you without colored lenses at all that is. It's a necessary part of moving forward, of moving past denial. This is a grieving process. And so, there may be anger, followed by bargaining, then sadness. But then the acceptance will come, and with acceptance we begin to move forward. We must tackle this work quickly and with dedication, for it's up to us to lead others forward.

RISE: A CALL TO THE LIGHT TRIBE

It's uncomfortable—I get that—to be still with our mirrors and to see what we see when we finally stare deeply in. Too uncomfortable perhaps, for most. The rush to return to a false normalcy seems to support that. And so the viruses of poverty, war, and late-stage capitalism spread hungrily onwards, each a pandemic all on its own, topped with an actual pandemic.

While some embraced the opportunity to return to lives that don't serve them well because it's easier to stay busy than to do the hard work of taking stock, others have become lost in the room or mirrors. It's possible to get trapped in the ugliness of what we see. And there is so much of it.

So how do we look into the darkness without allowing it to drown us—taking away from it what we need to do better and then returning to center? By looking from a place of love, for ourselves, for others, and by recognizing what the places we've been and the place we're now at have to teach us. As we see ourselves more clearly from a place of love, we begin to see each other with greater clarity and compassion. We become better reflections for one another in this holographic universe.

This is what's needed from us. Look around you at the ever-growing political divisions, at the worst in so many coming out. Look at the widespread refusal of so many amidst a pandemic to wear masks, or to care that cops are killing black people or that there are kids in cages, or to give a shit whatsoever about the suffering all around us. Let me say this about these people—that is their purpose. This era of contrasts is necessary. In the darkest darkness, the light can truly shine. It's an opportunity for those who choose to call the light home to embody their highest nature. So shine. Shine so brightly that those darkworkers remember that they chose to be that way, and they can choose the opposite at any moment as well.

CHAPTER 6. TAKING STOCK

Lightworkers and darkworkers are different sides of the same coin—beings who have chosen to embody different polarities. One is fueled by love and serves the collective; the other is fueled by fear and serves self. We are unbalanced, in a world of systems built to serve those in power are harming us all. But you see, darkworkers are just doing the job they signed up to do so that we may in turn play our part in this great re-balancing.

So we must be willing to see ourselves as those binary star systems—like suns orbiting black holes in an eternal dance with their dark twins, thanking them for dancing eternally with us, for allowing us to see ourselves for who we are, and reminding them that we were both born from and as stars. Let's dance friends, for it's time to take the lead.

Part 3
The War for Our Minds

Chapter 7
The Weaponization of Words

There is an invisible war raging all around us. It's a war for our minds. While this war has been raging for a long time now, sometimes these days it seems as if we're in the final battle. Our informational ecosystem feels a lot like a tornado, in which facts and false information are constantly swirling past us, and often otherwise intelligent and rational humans are grabbing indiscriminately, filling their minds with and constructing their lives around falsehoods designed to distract from what's really going on in our world.

Words are being weaponized like never before. As we pull back the veil for all of humanity, a shadowy evil parading as light is perpetrating a mass gas-lighting, inserting falsehoods into our collective narrative and calling them truth. As truth-seekers peel back layers from the onion, many are accepting what they find as "truth" because it's what they expect to find, but in reality, it's just misdirection.

RISE: A CALL TO THE LIGHT TRIBE

The stakes of this war are so much higher than our individual minds. The indigenous Andean people have a prophecy that originated a couple thousand years ago. It notes that humanity has taken two divergent paths throughout history. One is the path of the Eagle people, which is the path of the science and the logic. The second path is the path of the heart, compassion, and spirituality. It would be centuries before they met in the Fourth Pachacuti—a 500-year cycle, which on our calendar, began around 1500 CE/AD—around the time of Columbus, when the Eagle people decimated so many Condor people. Indeed, the Eagle nearly pushed the Condor towards extinction, as the prophecy predicted.

Then, the prophecy goes, 500 years later as the Fifth Pachacuti begins, the Eagle and Condor get the chance to fly a convergent path. In doing so, they can give birth to third species—a higher consciousness. This is where we now find ourselves. We are currently seeing the Eagle and Condor fly in a double-helix-like dance, feeling each other out, beginning to see themselves as two sides of the same coin, a balancing of dualities.

Werner Heisenberg, the German quantum mechanics pioneer who came up with the uncertainty principle, was right when he said, "The first gulp of the glass of natural sciences will turn you into an atheist, but at the bottom of the glass, God is waiting for you." Indeed, both science and spirituality are simply different angles for looking at the same thing. The age of polarity must end. This is the emergent union—finally—of the divine feminine with the divine masculine, who each, having healed their respective wounds, can again recognize each other as equal and sacred partners.

The world is divided as the current pandemic wages on, with the logic-based Eagle pushing the medical and pharmaceutical

CHAPTER 7. THE WEAPONIZATION OF WORDS

establishment as the path back to normalcy. Meanwhile, the heart-based Condor recognizes that the coronavirus is a message from Pachamama—Mother Earth—showing us everything that must change, as our "normal" is so broken, so that New Earth can coalesce.

Yet, there is a third player here, whose role is one of separation to prevent the Eagle and Condor from birthing their transformative offspring. If you adopt the religious understanding of good and evil as God and Satan, or if you're familiar with the concept of the "Lucifer Experiment" narrative (which says that God created Lucifer so that humans could experience separation and live out the endless possibilities created by free will within the entire spectrum between the duality of ultimate good and ultimate evil), then you might call this third player "Lucifer." This force works through human puppets in subtle but powerful ways, seeding the air with fallacies and theories based on "facts" that aren't, creating division between the Eagle and Condor. This is the enemy. Let us not be divided and conquered.

If Lucifer represents separation, including separation from truth, god is Ultimate Truth. Yes, this reality is nothing but a grand illusion, one that allows us the ability to experience embodied living in service of our souls' evolution. Yet, running over the divine mother matrix that creates this illusion are what can be described as overlaid matrices that create the many narratives of our world. Smaller truths lead to bigger truths, until you finally transcend the illusion.

When we run into a corrupted narrative—one based on falsehoods—and construct our lives and behavior according to false beliefs, we access a matrix that doesn't connect to any deeper truth matrix. We are separated from the path to Ultimate Truth.

RISE: A CALL TO THE LIGHT TRIBE

We are lost in the fog of confusion. These matrices are an assault on mass unity consciousness.

Too many narratives being propagated today, particularly among spiritual communities, are intellectually deceptive. That is, they contain fictional "facts" and use faulty reasoning to connect dots together that don't actually connect. Baseless conspiracy theories are being implanted with information that resonates with various strains of spiritual thought to make them easily palpable to those who are already more predisposed to believe information beyond what the scientific establishment has deemed to be true. It's a strategy designed to develop trust, so we don't dig very deeply. Do not drink the cherry-flavored arsenic simply because it's been labeled as medication and it tastes like other medicine.

Let me be clear here. I am not vilifying conspiracy theories. In fact, many have proven over time to be true. One of my favorites, and one of incredible relevance to this discussion, is MK-Ultra, the U.S. Central Intelligence Agency's secret experiments using psychedelics as psychological weapons to achieve mind control. What I warn against is corrupted information, leading us to mistruths, even when we think we're well informed because we've consumed a whole lot of content on any specific topic. Factual information can often serve as a bridge between different perspectives. In a time of such deep division, we more need bridges.

For instance, those who see vaccines as a way to keep people from dying from COVID-19 are not the enemy of those who see the dangers in a hastily developed vaccine created through a new and largely untried method (using a synthetic mRNA of the virus) and who rightly call out the many weird and potentially

CHAPTER 7. THE WEAPONIZATION OF WORDS

harmful ingredients that go into vaccines. Where one person sees potential for good, another may see the potential for harm. Both sides are valid—this is subjective reality. The enemy of both are the misinformation campaigns that obfuscate issues with lies and prevent honest discourse on such important topics. Beware of narratives that paint other everyday people, rather than corrupted and institutions systems, as the enemy.

Evil has encroached everywhere. Every last system, industry, and institution has been corrupted, including our information systems. Science is not the enemy. Spirituality is not the enemy. Pseudo-science and pseudo-spirituality are the enemies. Information on both sides is being manipulated to pit us against one another. It is thus up to each and every one of us to question everything, including ourselves, to root out beliefs based on dishonesty so that we do not unwittingly contribute to the enemy's cause. We must learn to put aside emotions when it comes to highly charged issues and become teachable when presented with information that erodes what we have decided is true.

I have devoted my career to the pursuit of truth—to discerning and sharing knowledge, or knowable truth, first as a news journalist and later as a publisher mostly of nonfiction, and calling bullshit when I see it both in my professional and personal lives. I am a voracious consumer of information with deep-seated trust issues and superb research and critical thinking skills. This is not me bragging. This is me telling you where my strength lies, so that you may allow yourself to really hear everything that I'm about to say. Please, allow me to teach you how to distill truth from the madness of our informational ecosystem, to see the false light for nothing more than man-made fluorescence. This is an act of love for my fellow man.

RISE: A CALL TO THE LIGHT TRIBE

Precisely as I write these pages, I have learned that a dear friend, mentor, and fairy godmother passed away. She was the only person I have ever met to share my passion for the art and science of truth. The symbolism of her passing is not lost on me. It was about two weeks before the news of her passing reached me that I realized that this book would not be complete without a chapter on discernment of truth, given the current state of our information ecosystem. Truth's fractal spirit left the material world as falsehoods metastasized in it. I hope to do her spirit justice in helping you fine-tune your discernment mechanisms in service of Ultimate Truth.

"In the beginning was the Word, and the Word was with God, and the Word was God," says the Bible, which also calls Jesus "Word made flesh." This is a concept of near-endless study in theology, but fields like quantum physics are beginning to look at the correlation between the quantum field (spirit), and vibration (word) as the egg and sperm of the material world. Let me put this another way: The storyteller creates the reality. In the information age, we are all potential storytellers, feeding a larger plot line. Well-told fallacies can change our beliefs, evoke emotions that become fuel for actions, distance us from facts, and diminish our ability to distinguish truth from falsehood. That's a well-studied phenomenon. Can you see then, why it's so important to understand what stories are creating distortion fields and feeding the false matrix, and why?

The information and instruction in the chapter that follows may make you uncomfortable. Yet, if we wish to win the war for our minds, we must do the difficult work of understanding our weapon and sharpening it for the battle that we are currently, whether we know it or not, fighting. Will you be a warrior or a pawn? May we allow our discomfort show us where our unwavering attention is needed.

Chapter 8
Becoming Guardians of Truth

*I*t might be tempting to think of truth in black-and-white terms; that something must be unequivocally either true or false, like the poles of duality. Unfortunately, truth is a far more complicated concept, and can be obfuscated by everything from our vantage point to our biology. Yet, being able to see through the smoke and past our biases is an essential skill for transcending illusion. Fortunately, that's a learnable skill, and I thank you for being here with me, willing to accept the information and do the work, because the power in our hands as individuals to transcend the flaws of our human brains to get above the murk, so to speak.

We will be using the words "truth" and "true" a lot here, so let's start with a basic question with a not-so-simple answer: What is truth? In other words, what makes something true? By definition, "truth" is that which coincides with fact or reality.

But you see, quantum physics now tells us that reality is subjective. In other words, two people looking at the same information, such as a set of facts, can interpret it differently to come to two distinct conclusions about the reality at which they are looking. Someone watching the sun set is experiencing a subjective reality. I see it going down. This is a reality for me. It is not an objective reality because not everyone is watching it set simultaneously. An objective truth is that we live on a planet that orbits the sun, and as the earth spins away from it, some people's view of the sun becomes obstructed based on their location on the planet. Semantics matter.

Remember, everything is vibration. Words are vibrations. Thoughts lead to words, which lead to reality. It's how we step from the quantum world—the place of everything and nothing—into the material world.

Given that subjective reality is more akin to perspective, rather than looking at subjective reality, let's focus on the building blocks of objective truth—facts. While subjective and objective reality may feel the same—they are encoded identically in our brains—objective truth is transcendental. It remains whether we are alive or not to understand it, and whether or not we choose to see it as such. In this way, it is a lot like love. In fact, I see them as twin rails of light on which we can travel into the upward dimensions.

A theory is a step up from opinion or belief, but is not truth either. Rather, it is a conceptual framework that attempts to explain something using logic and substantiated data. A theory can be proven to be true, assuming that the data on which it is based is valid. Yet, until that happens, we are relying on a type of faith, not knowing. We simply believe the thing in question to be true. This type of faith is what guides scientists to engage in relentless inquiry and experimentation.

CHAPTER 8. BECOMING GUARDIANS OF TRUTH

Even a fact or set of facts is not a truth. Sure, factual evidence can be woven together in logical arrangements to arrive at logically truthful conclusions. But factual evidence can also be woven illogically together into something that amounts to a falsehood. Both the quality of the information and the way in which it is woven with other pieces of information matter.

Without factual evidence, we can believe or feel something to be true, and we can understand that it can be true, but we cannot objectively know it to be true. To say that we know such a thing to be true is the ego talking. Breathe through the discomfort. A truth is true whether or not we know it to be, but it takes objectively factual evidence to make it a knowable truth.

Thus, factual information are the building blocks of knowable truth. We must be willing to put on our investigative caps, ask tough questions, and learn to seek answers from reliable sources. Are the things we are accepting as facts actually substantiated? Who and what we put our faith upon—the people and institutions presenting us with what they claim to be facts—must also come under scrutiny. We must understand the level of informational integrity the sources upon which we place our trust offer. Knowledge is power, so let us stand in our true power.

When evaluating information, four concepts—coherence, congruence, consistency, and usefulness—can get us on the road to discerning truthfulness. Does the information jive (or cohere) with everything that is known to be objectively true? Does our experience fit the objective facts (Is it congruent)? Do all the internal pieces fit elegantly (or consistently) together without contradicting one another? Does it provide the ability to apply a high degree of logic to our environmental circumstances, so that we can master our reality (Is it useful)? All four factors must be present for something to be objectively true.

Yet a truth can be true while another truth can be even truer. There are degrees to truth. Let me explain. A provisional true is one that, while being true today, may not hold true tomorrow in light of whatever new evidence may emerge. I like to think of provisional truth as Truth in the making. It can be accepted as likely and actionable, yet with the caveat that we not allow ourselves to become stuck on it should new and potentially contradictory facts come to light. This is the meaning behind Buddhist teacher Lin Chi's famous quote, "If you meet the Buddha on the road, kill him." When we feel we've found all the answers, we must look deeper, more carefully.

There is a complex science behind what we choose to accept as truth. Understanding how our brains process information can help us become better at discerning what information actually serves us, and what information is meant to distract us and turn us into pawns for the ministry of lies.

We may always find what we are looking for, even when those findings aren't supported by facts and logic. A person attached to a specific narrative will continue to find "evidence" in its support because what we seek is always seeking us too. But that's a bit like building a case based on circumstantial evidence. Attachment to a specific narrative can lead us into delusion, whereas non-attachment can lead us to clarity.

Non-attachment is tricky though, because our brains can attach to specific narratives without our express and conscious consent. So, as you'll see, understanding truth isn't just about looking at something external of us in a specific way, but also about understanding how our brains function.

CHAPTER 8. BECOMING GUARDIANS OF TRUTH

As human beings, we are full of fears, wishes, and programing, all of which usually lurk in the back recesses of our psyche, coloring our meaning-making process in ways that are difficult for us to see in ourselves. To "know thyself" is so much more complex than we might imagine.

Some researchers have looked at what makes us more likely to accept certain pieces of information as true over others, and why we might, when presented with factual information that contradicts what we have chosen to believe as true, double down on our false beliefs. Cognitive Scientists Hugo Mercier and Dan Sperber, who authored, "The Enigma of Reason," note that humans engage in reasoning primarily to justify what they already believe and convince others of their beliefs. This helps us create cooperation, but isn't a particularly helpful trait for actually finding truth.

Sometimes, we might come upon a piece of information that doesn't coincide with our world views, our understanding of reality, or other prior information that has resonated as true. We experience a sense of internal discomfort, and may conclude that the discomfort is our gut telling us that the new piece of information is false, when in fact the sense of discomfort is just cognitive dissonance, a type of mental conflict that occurs when we encounter information that runs contradictory to our beliefs, attitudes, and behaviors. We all experience this at some point; open-mindedness requires pushing through the discomfort.

Alternately, we may come across a piece of information that immediately sits well with us; it innately rings true. But why does it ring true? It may simply be that we've previously consumed the same or complementary information subconsciously, so when we do so consciously, we have an easy time accepting it as true; our brain has unwittingly been conditioned to do so.

RISE: A CALL TO THE LIGHT TRIBE

The brain is the sentient supercomputer within. It understands itself to live within our bodies, and so our preservation means its self-preservation. As such, it's not as concerned with the discernment of truth as it is with the assemblage of information in a way that makes being alive in this world most palatable for us.

The question then becomes, are we sufficiently resolute in our search for truth to deal with our discomfort, to do the sometimes difficult and time-consuming work of fact-checking the information we consume, evaluating the integrity of the sources producing it, and then engaging in critical thinking that takes into account the utilitarian workings of our brain? Or, will we simply accept the easy path and allow it to lead us wherever it may, even if that is astray?

This is why journalists deal in facts, putting many facts together to construct a version of the truth that most logical minds can agree upon. Traditionally, journalism has been the cornerstone of our informational ecosystem. It is why journalism in the United States has been dubbed "The Fourth Estate." The first three are the presidency, Congress, and the Supreme Court. The Fourth Estate is the unflinching look into the dealings of our government by journalists to give the public the information we need to vote in accordance with our best interests. It's a bit like commoditized shadow work.

Of course, all systems today have been corrupted. The world of "facts" is no different. It's not just that the victor controls the narrative; the control of the narrative makes the victor. But if we can understand the how of media corruption, we can discern the trustworthy from the deceitful. This is a rather secular topic; yet we are beings both of this world and fractal spirits of all that is, and sometimes the bridge to the spirit world is made

CHAPTER 8. BECOMING GUARDIANS OF TRUTH

by understanding the secular one. So, stay with me through what may seem like a departure from the spiritual towards the mundane. I assure you, crossing this bridge is a worthwhile endeavor. Like a scientist, let us look closely at the things we can see with our human eyes to find the things that are not yet within our view.

As a former journalist, I have met many professional journalists throughout my adult life. By and large, people who go into respectable journalism do so out of a sense of idealism that by providing objective knowledge about the world to people, they can help create a better world. They tend to be overeducated and under-paid helpers. Most adhere to the Society of Professional Journalists' Code of Ethics, which states that, "public enlightenment is the forerunner of justice...," and that "ethical journalism strives to ensure the free exchange of information that is accurate, fair and thorough, and that "an ethical journalist acts with integrity." Other codes for professional journalists share as common elements an oath of adherence to truthfulness via objectivity and accuracy, to impartiality via fair and balanced reporting, and to public accountability via transparency.

Journalists are trained to identify and put aside personal opinions, beliefs, and biases in pursuit of truth, while dissecting information to evaluate its verity. They make a living out of reporting the facts. Reporting false information or accepting bribes for any journalist at a reputable media outlet can lead to being blacklisted—in other words, an inability to continue making a living from journalism. It is thus in their best interests to be truthful. But, and you've probably guessed this much, individuals are rarely the big problem—it's the systems where the biggest opportunities for corruption lie.

RISE: A CALL TO THE LIGHT TRIBE

News organizations usually employ ombudsmen, whose job entails fostering self-criticism, advocating for adherence to professional standards, and ensuring accountability for the information being disseminated. Larger organizations may also employ fact-checkers, whose sole job is to analyze stories pre-publication to ensure every fact checks out as such. When fact-checkers aren't part of the reporter-to-consumer pipeline, editors take on the job of verifying information before it is published. For media outlets engaged in truth telling, their most valuable assets are the reliability of the information they disseminate, the level of professionalism with which they go about seeking and sharing information, and how accountable they allow themselves to be to the public. As with everything though, there are cracks. These are both the spaces where corruption creeps in and also the places where we can shine a bright light.

Media bias refers to the real or perceived bias of journalists and news organizations in how they select stories to cover and how to cover them. Media bias can cast serious doubt on the work of those working earnestly in the field. The problem stems from the fact that most media outlets today are part of large conglomerates with billionaires at the helm and large advertising contracts. Their business goals are making money and protecting stockholders' interests.

Yet board members, stockholders, and advertisers are not a constant, or even frequent, presence in newsrooms. By and large, newsrooms operate free of day-to-day corporate meddling. And they are led by people who care about truth. So much so, in fact, that they will make sure important stories get out, even if it's not through their employing company. Reporters have been known to find innovative ways to ensure people get the

CHAPTER 8. BECOMING GUARDIANS OF TRUTH

information they need to improve their lives. Reporters without Borders went as far as to establish The Uncensored Library, a server on the popular video game Minecraft, to circumvent news censorship in countries lacking freedom of the press and counter government disinformation campaigns meant to manipulate public opinion.

When Former President Donald Trump went to war with the press by calling reputable media outlets "fake news" because they shone a light on his incompetence and lies, he opened the door for anyone to decide that information was "fake news" if it doesn't support what they believe or hope to be true. Now is a good time for shadow work. We must take a good, hard look in the mirror if we want to be part of the solution, and not part of the problem. It's okay if this doesn't come naturally to you; I will give you the tools to do so. Push through with me.

The trend of labeling actual news "fake" when it's convenient to do so does not only present a form of mind control; it is also an affront to freedom of expression and information worldwide. When journalists who are reporting facts and shedding light on abuses are not believed, we as a society become ineffective at opposing those societal ills that keep humanity in this density, including inequalities of all kinds; crimes against the Earth; genocide and the torture of activists and prisoners of conscience; and the safeguarding of children and animals who cannot stand up for themselves.

Allowing our brains to fall prey to thinking that something is "fake news" because it doesn't fit into our worldview also makes us easy pawns much more likely to fall for actually false information. And we need to be aware of the ease with which our brains do this, because fake news does exist. And we have been called to be protectors of the very concept of Truth.

RISE: A CALL TO THE LIGHT TRIBE

AllSides.com defines "fake news" as "journalism or information that either deliberately or unintentionally misleads people and distorts reality by spreading false information, hoaxes, propaganda, or misrepresentation of facts." Fake news, it explains, "can be used as propaganda or marketing tactic, as a way to fairly or unfairly discredit ideological opponents, or as a way to increase revenue via engagement metrics such as clicks, views, comments, likes and shares."

The solution is of course, to understand where sound information is flowing from, and to learn to see the puppet strings so that we can eliminate that which does not serve Truth. Keep the baby, but toss the bathwater. What do media scholars have to say about where you get your information and why?

Only by getting intimately acquainted with a source of information is it really possible over time to develop a sense of their level or truthfulness and integrity. However, being a good fact-checker never hurts. Organizations devoted to fact-checking information, like Snopes.com, FactCheck.org, and PolitiFact can make that task easier. May we all dig deep when we find ourselves too readily accepting or rejecting a piece of information. Who are the sources being cited? What are their qualifications? Does their professional history point to a high level of integrity? In other words, is it likely that they really know what they claim to know, and should they be trusted? Who and what are they affiliated with? What do they stand to gain or lose by being outspoken about whatever it is they're speaking on or against? Always follow the money in all directions: Who is funding them? And what do they gain and from who by saying what they are saying? What personal biases or position of privilege could be clouding their minds?

CHAPTER 8. BECOMING GUARDIANS OF TRUTH

In 2016, Italian researchers who wanted to see just how gullible we can be on social media planted fake news to see how and how far the misinformation was spread. What they found is disturbing. We are more likely to comment, like, and share conspiracy theories than factual information. And such content has serious, real-world implications. Consider that in 2016, a man shot up a Washington, D.C. pizza restaurant because he bought the conspiracy theory that the restaurant served as the headquarters of a pedophile ring involving Hillary Clinton. His inability to decode fact from fiction turned him into a pawn of the mind-control puppet masters. Confusion can kill. We saw this after the 2020 elections at the U.S. capitol, when right-wing insurgents who believed the narrative created by the illusion-maker known as Q-Anon stormed the building, some intending to kidnap and kill lawmakers who opposed Trump.

This subtle and subversive mind control goes a little like this: The puppet master casts doubt on the pipelines of truth, while simultaneously fueling pipelines of lies, so when we turn away from truth they have labeled as fake news, the alternate informational fire hoses to which we turn are actual falsehoods. These falsehoods they feed us may feel maybe more real for a couple of reasons.

For one, they are cushioning their lies with truth—the best liars always do. Just as the devil hides behind the cross, so too does the liar hide behind the truth. Second—and this is super important—our psyche will want to buy into what the puppet masters are selling more than the actual truth. Why? The truth of our collective situation is so multifaceted and complex. There are so many facts and so many different ways to view those facts. It is difficult to be well informed and to then find ways in which our

RISE: A CALL TO THE LIGHT TRIBE

actions can be part of the solution. It's easier to buy into simple narratives with clear bad guys and a white knight who we have simply to wait for to ride in and save the day.

It's worth acknowledging too that our brains have been called upon to handle an unprecedented and ever-increasing volume of facts since the Internet and 24-hour cable news became part of nearly every household. And social media has made us part of the news, or at the very least culturally mandating that we have an opinion on every fact (and lie-as-fact) that comes across our screen. We have not been able to intellectually adapt to this informational inundation; it happened too quickly.

Let me put this in more real-world terms. The Internet poster who goes by the handle Q-Anon is the source of many conspiracy theories masquerading around the Internet as alternative facts. The narrative is cushioned with talk of The Great Awakening, which so many of us see actually happening with our own two eyes; news of pedophilia rings (allegedly controlled by the Democratic Party), which are and have been a thing for nearly as long as humans have been around; and tales of "mole children," who are allegedly kept in underground tunnels by the world's elite for the purpose of harvesting their adrenochrome, which, depending on different versions of this story, is ingested by the rich to give them a high, keep them young, or for use in Satanic rituals. These children, blind and deformed from so many years underground, were to be rescued by a force led by Former President Trump in what was dubbed "The Storm." Except it never happened—just as the world never ends on the many previously prophesied dates—and the story simply gets revamped and recycled when a new, hell-bent but charismatic leader appears.

CHAPTER 8. BECOMING GUARDIANS OF TRUTH

Let's dissect this a bit. "Q" famously posted this on an Internet forum called 4Chan, and later on another named 8Chan. It should be noted that these boards are famously the online dens of young, irrational, and angry white young men, some of whom have posted their deranged manifestos on these forums before going on killing sprees. Someone who is clearly a bad guy—the same racist, sexist, ableist former president who put children in cages; pushed people into going back to work amidst a pandemic even as the number of deaths rose because his billionaire pals lost more money; and gutted the Environmental Protection Agency while also auctioning off public lands to major polluters—was portrayed as the white knight. His opponents—the Democrats—were of course portrayed as evildoers.

Given that sex trafficking is such a problem, and that society in general can rally against pedophilia, it makes perfect sense to center the narrative on exploited children. For those of us who are sick of watching the world go to hell, it offers some hope to which we can cling while simultaneously and subconsciously sticking our heads in the sand when it comes to what is actually going on. I mean, what a mixture—spirituality, politics, exploited children, and celebrities. It's a well-constructed fabrication, but it's just a fabrication, if not directly by Trump's people, then by his supporters or Russia as part of its ploy to dismantle the United States. And in fact, researchers have tracked such conspiracy theories back to Russian troll farms—buildings full of people being paid by the Russian government to disseminate information meant to distract and befog the American public. "Hey, hey! Look over here, while I do this over there!"

The danger with such rabbit holes is that they present a group of "dots" that are passed as facts, when only some may be facts. But it's easy to say that if A and B are facts, then C and D must be as well. In other words, we establish credibility through sequential rather than randomized spot-checks. We are all doing our best to get through the day, often with more obstacles than we can handle. Our lack of bandwidth for deep truth-seeking in a survival-based reality makes us easy prey. As a result, we accept all the dots as facts and follow them down a rabbit hole to conclusions that are, at least at the beginning, false. And we become invested in those conclusions, because in the connecting dots that have been strategically placed for our finding, we believe ourselves to have independently seen the light when we've just been subtly manipulated. We haven't "done our research," but merely followed carefully-placed arrows to strategically-determined locations.

But now that a specific narrative is out there and being shared far and wide, it's only a matter of time before it becomes fact, as someone with the wherewithal to see if adrenochrome is truly an elixir of youth or the ultimate psychedelic finds and a penchant for crime decides to exploit children, thus proving the narrative true at some future point. If even a portion of these conspiracy theories become true when they weren't true to begin with, may it not be because we had a hand in creating that reality through belief in the lies of others.

Yet sadly, it is often those screaming "fire" the same ones setting the fires. Even as I write this book, a devout follower of Q's #saveourchildren distraction campaign was arrested for murdering a baby. Do you see the parallels between that and Trump condemning Mexicans as rapists and murderers while simultaneously raping the Earth and leading to countless U.S. deaths from a botched COVID-19 response? The #saveourchildren ploy was easy to see as such because the people rallying behind it

CHAPTER 8. BECOMING GUARDIANS OF TRUTH

were not the ones protesting the kids in cages; they merely wanted to be seen as being righteously outraged, except it was an outrage that cared only about kids that looked like them, and only to the extent that nothing was required of them to actually save said kids.

We are seeing an alternate reality game played on a massive scale, where we are the unwilling players. Wikipedia describes an "alternate reality game" as "an interactive networked narrative that uses the real world as a platform and employs transmedia storytelling to deliver a story that may be altered by players' ideas or actions." A networked narrative or distributed narrative is one that is "partitioned across a network of interconnected authors, access points, and/or discrete threads." Rather than being driven by a specificity of details, the details "emerge through a co-construction of the ultimate story by the various participants or elements." The defining characteristics of ARGs are "intense player involvement with a story that takes place in real time and evolves according to the players' responses" and "characters that are actively controlled by the game's designers."

Are you beginning to understand now? Do you get how a false narrative by one person strategically placed on one Internet board and picked up by others across various platforms can spread like wildfire, evolving as different people add their individual opinions and attempt to connect additional dots to the narrative? Individual meaning-making efforts have been hijacked to sell the masses on false narratives to distract from the real ones.

This is how the Holocaust became possible. Adolf Hitler was a master propagandist who devised the "fake news" strategy while simultaneously pushing his version of reality. He literally wrote the book on this strategy. "The key to understanding why many Germans supported him lies in the Nazis' rejection of a rational, factual world," wrote Benjamin Carter Hett as part of a study on Hitler. Is it any surprise then, that as Former President Trump's lawyers asked that he receive unprecedented immunity from prosecution, a Russian, state-backed television station pushed the wacky narrative that Bill Gates is responsible for the COVID-19 pandemic, drawing on various equally-wacky online sources. "Hey, hey, look over here (while we do this over there)!"

As the masses consume such alternate reality narratives, we alter our beliefs and behaviors according to strategically constructed lies. And, believing ourselves "woke" to true events, we may shout what we believe from the rooftops, this amplifying the puppet master's message. We can become puppets in this great deception.

Yes, vaccines save lives by preventing pandemics, and also yes, they are loaded with dubious chemicals that sometimes cause very serious health problems in certain individuals and should be subject to stringent safety testing and reporting. Yes, there is considerable evidence that 5G may be harmful to humans and animals and should be carefully studied before widespread implementation. And yes, it's always wise to question the motives on the ultra-rich whose actions have the potential to significantly impact our world. Yet, to believe that all of these are somehow connected and to devote our attention to such wild narratives, while the government quietly moves to criminalize fossil fuel protests and empower rhetoric of division and hate is to fall under control of the puppet masters vying for dominance of our world by first swaying the minds of the masses. Let us not be led like lemmings into a fog concealing a precipice.

Trump was not the problem. He was one of many world leaders playing from the same game book. And none of them

CHAPTER 8. BECOMING GUARDIANS OF TRUTH

are the problem. They are the result of the problem—of the uncontrollable greed that has created billionaires and trillionaires while most of us live out a form of indentured servitude to capitalist masters, and where we may fall prey to all forms of schemes to divide us so that we are too busy fighting one another to see the real enemy clearly. We are all—good guys and bad—method actors in a play that has already been written. Yet, if we signed up to play a specific role, like that of a lightworker, we should know how to play that role well, and do everything in our power to do so. That includes being able to see clearly, to not be unwittingly made into a pawn of the opponent.

In his book, Conversations with God, Neale Donald Walsh writes "I have sent you nothing but angels," a message channeled from source. I understand that in two distinct but complementary ways. This duality-based existence may be full of what seem like monsters, yet these too are simply method actors whose roles allow us the often-painful gift of seeing what we do not want. And we are not alone at the mercy of these seeming "monsters." We live in a world constructed by the cumulative work of countless artists, healers, teachers, scientists, and others dedicated to making life better, and we benefit in many ways, large and small, on a daily basis from those who came before us and those sharing space with us now.

I hope that feels as true to you as it does to me. Speaking of such, where does intuition and claircognizance fit into the discussion on truth and reality? What about tapping into the information swirling all around us in the unified field? What about trusting what our gut tells us to be true? We've often been led to believe that you can't walk both paths—the scientific and spiritual—at the same time; that we must choose one. But there is simply no need for that.

RISE: A CALL TO THE LIGHT TRIBE

We should not discount intuition and claircognizance, and science is finally beginning to look less skeptically upon these. Yet because intuition, claircognizance, and false intuition can sometimes feel almost identical, it can be too tempting to either accept all of it as valid or all of it as invalid, when really all that's needed is some careful discernment.

Let's start with the difference between real and false intuition. False intuition originates in our brains as the result of imperceptible yet fallible background processes that are happening all the time. We live in a chaotic world. As a result, our brains are constantly—whether we realize it or not—trying to identify patterns and connect distinct pieces of information, so that we can determine the best way to move about in the world. But sometimes, the information being pulled into this process is flawed in some way, if not flat-out false. The subconscious mind is not analytical, after all.

Like fish swimming through water, all of this so-called evidence passes imperceptibly through our personal culturescapes. These are the implicit and unconscious biases, beliefs, and attitudes shaped by our personal experiences, cultural programming, and membership in certain classes (e.g., race, gender, etc.). The culturescape is as invisible to us as the air we breathe. Our subconscious brains then use reasoning to tie it all together.

Unfortunately, human reasoning is not always logical. In 1994, Seymour Epstein, an emeritus professor of psychology at the University of Massachusetts-Amherst, conducted an experiment in which people were asked to pick a red jelly bean from jars containing either 10 or 100 beans. Most of the beans in both jars were white. The 10-bean jar had just one red bean, while the 100-bean jar held seven red beans. Participants' statistical odds were better if choosing from the 10-bean jar (10 percent versus 7 percent

CHAPTER 8. BECOMING GUARDIANS OF TRUTH

for the 100-bean jar). More participants intuitively reached for the 100-bean jar, falsely reasoning that more red beans to pick from would increase their chances of grabbing a red bean, though this was not the rational choice.

The results of our subconscious processes are conclusions that can be easily mistaken for gut feelings but are really just a hodge-podge of information that our brains have imperfectly stitched together to try to make sense of the world. Our brains like order, so this resulting understanding of reality can resonate as real on a very deep level.

The world is a crazy, chaotic place. It is natural to want to take all of these troubling dots, connect them into a single narrative that makes some sense, and tie a big bow around them. It is, after all, the point of intuition to help us figure out our environment so that we can know the best way to proceed in this seemingly random world. Engaging in this kind of flawed meaning-making is human, and we all do it. Yet, in an informational ecosystem that is replete of falsehoods and people who stand to gain by pushing the narratives that serve their agendas, we can unwittingly be stitching a narrative with the equivalent of degraded thread. And because we want whatever narrative we arrive at to be true—because as troubling as it may seem, at least it makes sense—we are instantly biased in its favor, so we seek out and accept only further information that serves our confirmation bias.

What's more, sharing the narrative we've decided is true can feel like the right thing to do, not just for ourselves, but also to help others come to the same understanding we feel have benefited us. As a result, we become unwitting bishops in disseminating mistruths.

To be clear, real intuition is helpful; false intuition is not. Real intuition is felt in the body, not the brain as the result of subconscious data processing. If what feels like intuition comes in response to something that has caused us fear or worry, it's probably not real intuition, just our very active brains trying to make meaning out of things.

Likewise, if, upon consuming a piece of information, our initial response is "Ah-ha! I knew it," maybe we don't. That's the brain, through which our egos speak. And if we feel ourselves invested in an outcome proving us right, it may not be real intuition, but rather something more akin to wishful thinking and highly susceptible to confirmation bias.

Pure intuition should make us feel open, relaxed, excited, and curious. It should make us want to dig deep to learn more. False intuition, on the other hand, can make us feel as if we've got things figured out; it's an open and shut case, and no one with a differing opinion can tell us otherwise.

The research on intuition and claircognizance has led to sometimes-contradictory findings. I believe the reason for that is that researchers do not differentiate false intuition (which comes as the result of subconscious brain-based process) from real intuition and claircognizance (which do not originate in the brain). I don't objectively know this to be true, but believe it to be so based on my own study of this subject over many years and my personal experience.

Claircognizance is like intuition on steroids, and works in much the same way. We don't just have gut feelings, but rather a feeling of inner knowing of something there is no rational reason for us to know. For me, claircognizance shows up completely out of nowhere, or the now-here. It feels more mind-based than brain-based. It's not an "ah-ha!" kind of moment because there often is no prior thought devoted to the topic at hand nor prior exposure to related content. We can test information that comes

CHAPTER 8. BECOMING GUARDIANS OF TRUTH

via claircognizance by digging for factual information that either supports or debunks that information.

Because it can be easy to confuse the mind and the brain, it can also be easy to confuse claircognizance for brain-based processes. Our brains are the physical organs housed in your heads, whereas the mind, though associated with the brain, is not confined to it. False claircognizance can be information previously stored in our subconscious and brought to the surface by our brains or through the insightful interpretation of information. Claircognizance, on the other hand, originates outside your brain. You are observing the information as it exists in the quantum realm rather than creating it.

Both intuition and claircognizance are developable skills. Our bodies are antennas, all capable of this. As we get better at identifying brain-centered processes, ego, and wishful thinking, and separating them from the equation, we become an open channel to receive information from the unified field, rather than from the rest of the material world.

A couple of strategies that work to put me in the correct state of mind to access information from the unified field involve using meditative (slow and measured) breathing while manipulating the focus of my eyes. I find that using my peripheral vision on both sides simultaneously but not actually focusing on anything seems to inform the unified field that I am receptive to whatever information it wants me to have. This technique is like picking up the phone to communicate with the quantum field. The longer you hold the gaze, the longer the phone conversation lasts. The second technique involves finding the spot where the ceiling and wall of whatever room I am in meet, then drawing my eyes back about a foot away from that joint, towards me, and holding in meditation for as long as possible. This opens an interdimensional

RISE: A CALL TO THE LIGHT TRIBE

portal of sorts, through which our higher selves can more clearly communicate with us, leading to very useful intuitions.

With both intuition and claircognizance, it's important to understand that the ego can lead us to believe that we are experiencing the real thing when we're actually not. So, we must test our instrument to learn how well calibrated it is, and do so frequently, as the ego is always waiting for the right opportunity to sneak in.

Jules Henri Poincare, a French mathematician, theoretical physicist, engineer, and scientific philosopher who died in the early 1900s, once said, "it is through science that we prove, but through intuition that we discover." So, let us be guided down the road of ideas by intuition, yet use our analytical minds to discern truth from falsehoods, so that our attention and behavior may be well aligned with who we say we are.

Part 4
We're Who We've Been Waiting For

Chapter 9
Laying Our Old Selves to Rest

*I*t's impossible as I write this to not reflect on the state of the world. How much more brokenness will it take for us to get out of our own way and step into who we're meant to be and what we're here to do?

A pandemic rages on. Economies are faltering. The war machine rolls onwards. There is plastic in even our water. Many animals face extinction. Millions of people face a grim future. Protests over racial inequalities and industries that cause irreversible pollution have left the downtrodden and their allies, more than anything, exhausted. A long and brutal winter is upon us.

This is the tiniest tip of the iceberg, as so much calamity and destruction is going on in the world today that it would require an entire book to list all the ways in which we are self-destructing. It's never been so clear just how many of the big systems that make up our society do not serve us, and quite the contrary, are tools of violence and oppression.

CHAPTER 9. LAYING OUR OLD SELVES TO REST

Meanwhile, people are so divided, between those fighting the systems of oppression and those fighting for the survival of those systems, because it's all they've ever known, because they lack the imagination to help create a better world, or because they have been so deeply programmed to support those systems. All this while the constant evils of the world rage on, from war and human trafficking to the torture and slaughter of innocent animals. Is it too much yet? Have we reached our limit?

There is so much pain and so much chaos, so much ugliness that may feel like the exact opposite of who we are, or try to be. Yet, we must not look away. Now is a time for collective shadow work, and to use what is happening outside of us to more clearly see inwards. We are our own creators, and this is how we remake ourselves as greater beings than we currently are; by shining light into all of our dark places. So, let's summon the courage it takes to do this work, for it must be done. May we embrace the chrysalis as a vehicle for transformation, so that when we emerge, it is not as caterpillars but as beautiful butterflies.

In Jungian psychology, the "shadow" refers to the unconscious aspects of our personality that the conscious ego does not identify with. It is the side of us that we keep hidden in the shadows, often even from ourselves. We have disowned that part of ourselves because it doesn't coincide with the version of us we've chosen to embody. All of us have shadows, and shadow work to do.

"How can I be substantial if I do not cast a shadow? I must have a dark side also if I am to be whole," said Carl Jung, the founder of analytical psychology. To cast light on our shadows is to acknowledge more of us, to call in more of our power, and to live from a place of nonduality. On the other hand, to ignore our shadows is to allow ourselves to be susceptible to all that we have disowned, for those traits are always peering out just behind the corner. It is why so often, we are our own worst enemies.

We may have an easy time identifying the things outside of us that we don't like in others, and more generally, in the world, yet have blinders preventing us from seeing how those things are, in one way or another, a part of us too. What is outside us is within us. As above, so below. This is why shadow work is the most sacred work any human being can undertake. As we change ourselves, we reflect a higher vibration out into the world.

Finding our shadows requires understanding that everything outside us is a reflection of something within us. We must be willing to take a hard and humbling look in the mirror. "Wait, wait," you may say, "that can't be true. There are things I see in certain others, that are most definitely not a part of who I am." No, friend. Look deeper. Look longer. Change the angle from which you look into the mirror. We must not let the discomfort of our cognitive dissonance keep us from this sacred work.

A 2,500-year-old collection of books unearthed in Egypt contained, among other things, the original books of the Bible that were left out of the New Testament when Emperor Constantine condensed that part of the Bible in the fourth century. One book, The Book of Thomas, which is thought to consist of the teachings of Jesus as they were dispensed and received by the scribe, talks about three mirrors. These mirrors are a toolkit for doing shadow work, explains Author-Scholar Gregg Braden. You see, the shadow self is good at hiding. Sometimes you have to change your angle.

The three mirrors can be applied to anything upon which you wish to shed light within yourself. Whatever you see external of you, look for within you. Imagine a world in which everyone

CHAPTER 9. LAYING OUR OLD SELVES TO REST

looked deeply at their darkness, seeking to understand it and love it whole. It's the equivalent of coaxing a feral kitten from a ditch with milk and a warm blanket.

The mirror of the moment is the first mirror discussed in this book. It's probably the mirror you've heard discussed. It says that our environment is a reflection of who we are. The second mirror shows us the things we judge. What does our judgment tell us about ourselves? The third mirror shows us the parts of us that we have compromised or given away—the things we're subsequently lacking. This is the most complex of the mirrors. Sometimes, it's what makes others attractive to us; they have the pieces we are subconsciously missing. We surround ourselves with joyous people, for instance, because we have lost our joy, or with talkative people because we've silenced our own voice. This mirror isn't always so kind though. For instance, some of us have wished to be more forgiving, having known bitterness for some circumstance or another, so we are presented with people who give us the opportunity to forgive, by hurting us.

Ultimately, mirror work brings us into a state of unity, of seeing our oneness through our diversity. We are to love our enemies, and forgive those blinded by hatred and apathy, because ultimately, we are all shards of the same mirror reflecting back to each other different parts of ourselves. We all have been, in some way and at some time, ignorant. We all have been, in some way and at some time, blind to our true oneness. We must stand in solidarity with one another. It's the only way out of this mess. Shadow work is the foundation of sacred activism, for once we befriend ourselves fully, we become allies of those who need allyship. This is how movements happen.

As the world devolves into further chaos and violence, I see people uniting to create a better, more equitable world, and I see those vibrating at a lower frequency attempting to sow discord and incite violence. It's beautiful and horrifying all at once. It's the phoenix diving down, aflame, so that it can rise from the ashes, a better version of itself. Will you embody the phoenix, casting spotlights on your shadows to create a better reflection? Be relentless in your inquiry until finally, you see your shadows clearly, looking back at you.

Sometimes the shadows are what we expect, and sometimes they surprise us. And then? Then we hold our shadow's hand lovingly and bring it into the full light of day, and we forgive ourselves until there is only love where darkness once lurked. Looking in the mirror is rarely pleasant, but it's necessary if we want to be a part of the solution, of creating a better world.

We must hold not only ourselves, but also each other, accountable, as swords sharpening one another in the fire. It is a lack of accountability that has allowed so much evil to be perpetrated in the world—those with power threading on the backs of those without it—for some sort of gain. Social justice is not a thing of the world, it's a thing of the spirit. To stand as allies and guardians of our fellow brothers and sisters, of plants and animals, and of Gaia herself, is to walk in the footsteps of Archangel Michael. As Dr. Martin Luther King, Jr. said, "Power at its best is love implementing the demands of justice, and justice at its best is power correcting everything that stands against love."

The solution is love—courageous, supportive, accountability-focused love. As I send love inwards and outwards, the chrysalis cracks further. Someone new is emerging. And I see more clearly, that there is no difference between outward and inward. We are a soup of self-replicating material in flux, of molecules crashing, breaking apart and recombining. Destruction and creation

CHAPTER 9. LAYING OUR OLD SELVES TO REST

are happening simultaneously within us, exactly as they are happening outside of us.

So let us mourn the old world, for it is gone and going. Let us further mourn our old selves, for indeed, we have been through the fire and in it have been forged into something new, into leaders and teachers and healers; into beings who create rather than destroy, who love rather than hate, who understand rather than judge.

Grief is a natural response to all that we have witnessed, to all that we have been a part of and a party to. It is okay to look back on our former selves, to see how we have in some way, been part of the problem, yet love ourselves enough to know that at every step, like everyone else, we were just doing our best to survive the incredibly hostile conditions of embodied living on this planet. Be the parent to yourself that you wish you'd had. Practice self-forgiveness often. Cradle your inner child. But also hold yourself accountable for being true to your highest self. When we do that, we stand fully in our power.

Maybe most of all, understand that healing happens in layers, on its own time. We can help it along, and forward leaps may leave us pleasantly surprised, while backward slides may catch us unprepared. It's all part of the process. Some days, I look in the mirror and find myself in awe of how much I've changed, how much more clarity I have, and how much more on-purpose my life is than just a couple short years ago. On those days, I can't help but smile at the woman I see in the mirror. Other days, sometimes in the middle of random mundane tasks, the enormity of all I've lost and grieved comes rushing back.

You know what, though? There is so much power in grief, in the knowledge that despite what you may have gone through, what you may have lost, here you are standing, all the wiser for the

RISE: A CALL TO THE LIGHT TRIBE

wear. I stand here with all of the skills and all of the scars I needed to acquire to become a version of me who remembers that I came here to teach, to build, and to lead. The journey has been difficult, but the destination is worth it.

And so we find ourselves at a funeral of sorts, having lived through the death of the old, and raising our heads through our tears to envision what life will look like from here on out even as the casket is lowered into the ground—and maybe while, all around us, actual caskets are being interred. May we remember that death is nothing but a doorway, and may we step through our metaphorical deaths completely unafraid.

Chapter 10
Emerging from the Chrysalis

*T*he world may continue to burn around us. Yet, the new begins to emerge too. The light entering through the cracks in the shell may seem blinding and harsh as the chrysalis breaks apart; if it didn't, the butterfly's wings would never flutter through the air on a warm, sunny day.

If everything happening in the world and even in your personal life today seems like some surreal post-apocalyptic plot, it's because this is where we find ourselves. Merriam-Webster's online dictionary defines "post-apocalyptic" as a world "existing or occurring after a catastrophically destructive disaster or apocalypse," where "nature has become just as violent as humanity."

I propose that we collectively decide that the many catastrophes we have brought upon one another and upon Gaia and all of the non-human beings who call her home were the apocalypse. It has already happened. Our friends in the animal and plant world would likely agree. We have allowed the lungs of our planet to burn, killing millions if not billions of living beings; we have polluted and over-fished our oceans and rivers, turning them into liquid deserts; and we have perpetrated untold acts of cruelty and violence against ourselves, the beings who share this planet with us, and the planet itself.

We are part of nature, and like an invasive virus, we have ravaged this planet. So as we reflect chaos and destruction onto our environment, our environment is now reflecting that back to us. Just look around. This is the post-apocalypse.

I write this not to be grim, but to offer that we can collectively decide that the worst has already happened; that the beginning is not only near, but that it is here now. We need not continue to simply watch in horror as the world burns to ashes. The world may be burning to ashes, but as it burns, another is being birthed, a better world that requires us to emerge from the fire anew, to lead the way for others, setting a better example and charting a new course.

So I plead with you. Let us collectively agree that the turning point has been reached. Because if we do not, calamities will continue to happen. The multi-sided fun-house mirror will continue to dish up horror and despair. Will it take another world war? Total nuclear destruction? The complete eradication of bees? I choose to imagine that we are past that; that we are not so dense as to find ourselves there.

Yet, this mudslide may well continue, if not for our collective dedication to say, "No more. It stops with me," and to back that up with action. That calls for commitment to relentless self-inquiry and accountability. We are not insignificant. Through our example, we create ripples of change that disperse ever wider, and

CHAPTER 10. EMERGING FROM THE CHRYSALIS

the people whose lives we touch and inspire through our examples create their own ripples, and it all compounds until critical mass is reached and this ship of ours makes a wide turn.

Think back on our conversation about conspiracy theories and alternate reality games. This is the same concept. Rather than allow our fear to fuel potential realities that do not serve us, we are in a unique position to imprint onto the universe the reality we'd rather experience. Help me hack the matrix. Believe that the change you want to see is already here. See New Earth rising with me, and she *will* rise.

This takes transcending our fear, and having the courage to dance with joy for the new beginning we're in a position to give ourselves. We are free to manifest the collective future of our dreams if we're willing to dream together while awake.

When you look back on this moment right now one day, what will you see in hindsight? Will you like what you see? Did you do the work required of you to become the truest expression of your soul? Were you a part of the solution? Allow the chrysalis to crack open; this is the signal that the transformation is complete. You are everything you've known yourself to be, and so much more.

If you're reading this, you are on time. We are on time. We've walked through the fire so that we might show others the way through; so that we can be waiting at the other end with water as our fellow human beings begin to awaken, to pass through the fires of their own blessed destruction so that they may recreate themselves in their original, divine image.

They say Jesus died on the cross for our sins. What if our core wounds, those wounds we suffer early in life that make our truest selves withdraw and our egos take the lead, are the

RISE: A CALL TO THE LIGHT TRIBE

original sin? Look around you. So much of the ills humanity and the planet are experiencing are a direct result of ego-led living. When we metaphorically put our egos on the cross through unflinching self-inquiry, compassion and forgiveness for ourselves and others, and gratitude for the opportunity to be a part of this amazing journey, we rise again as divine beings of light, with the ability to transform our world for the better of all. Jesus led by example; he taught us how to transcend ourselves to be of service to all of humanity. We too are here to lead by example. And it's time to lead.

Enough of us are formed and awake within our chrysalises. We are ready to break free and burst into flight. Though we may not yet know what flight looks like—nor imagine it really—it's what we're built for and the only thing left is the doing of it. Trust that the air will hold you up as the wings you've created for yourself unfurl around you. May we shed the layers of self-doubt and old-world programming like pieces of broken chrysalis as new butterflies taking our first flight.

Chapter 11
The Great Work Ahead

*L*ight and dark, good and evil. Those contrasts seem ever glaring today, as the old world falls away and glimpses of New Earth begin to surface. In some ways, it may seem like duality is winning. In fact, all that is happening is that the veil is lifting. The veil itself is becoming more apparent. Let us welcome this development with joy, because we can address what we can identify. It takes understanding the separation to choose unity. It takes acknowledging the darkness to walk in light.

We fall through densities to come into these bodies. Pure spirit—the stuff of which the void that is all around us is made—becomes soul through the infusion of akasha, our lived experiences through many eons. At a soul level, we are our stories. Yet, we are not just souls. We are embodied beings, born of the marriage of soul to matter. It's a marriage consecrated by breath. We are shaped not only by our akashic records but also by the information passed down from our ancestors and stored in our cells, both prior to and after birth.

RISE: A CALL TO THE LIGHT TRIBE

It is our sacred mission to learn how to live in bodies as if we are pure spirit, transcending the many ways in which we are separated and divided from all that is. This is the core work of ascension. Ancient mystery schools taught this using the tree of life sacred geometry. The bottom portion represents embodied being, the middle section is pure soul, and the top section is spirit and oneness with all there is. We then, are here to climb up that tree. We are not only ascending, but are also in charge of our own ascension.

Many of us feel an inner knowing of having incarnated in this time and space for specific reasons. Some of us, for instance, have agreed to be healers, teachers, way showers, dreamers, builders—all ultimately here in service to humanity and Gaia. Others are here with no other purpose than to shine so brightly that they remind others of who they are. We may be a species with amnesia, but as more of us begin remembering, we trigger others into remembrance.

As we learn to walk in our bodies as spirit—threading gently upon this planet and walking kindly alongside other living beings—we remember ourselves more. And we level up too. The universe responds to our efforts. It gives us a hand up when it sees us actively working to climb that sacred tree of life, or walk the cobbled road. Miracles happen when we commit to living as miracles.

It doesn't matter whether you know why you're here. It matters that you show up to do the work. When you take one step, even if you can't see the road ahead of you, the next step appears. I am not saying it's easy. But that's part of becoming a peaceful warrior—doing the good things even when they're difficult. That is how we cultivate willpower, dedication, and grit.

CHAPTER 11. THE GREAT WORK AHEAD

It can be too easy to get lost in the everyday doings of being a human, to be so busy that we don't stop to reach that still point, where connection with our highest self and with all there is can be reached. Yet, this is an essential starting point. If you do nothing else, adopt a meditation practice.

There are many ways to meditate. Don't worry about first finding out which is right for you. Start where it's easiest, whether that's using a guided meditation or simply sitting in silence and allowing your mind to clear. The road will open before you as you go. You'll find what works for you and what doesn't. Borrow and combine techniques as you see fit to create a meditation method that is all your own.

The important thing is that you show up. This is not only how you begin to remember, but also how you can open yourself to receive direction and send intention into the void. Pick up the phone receiver. Meditation also has countless benefits beyond the spiritual, from helping us become more creative, leading to powerful insights about problems we may be facing, and even allowing us to rewrite our own DNA to heal ailments and access new gifts.

Over time, I have found meditation to be critical for helping me live each moment in the now; for creating space between the doing and the being, infusing everything I do with a mindfulness that wasn't there before. And that's really the key for ascension, isn't it? Because spirit doesn't live in a body that has to wake up, go to work or school, make meals, shower, and sleep, etc. Spirit just is. When we can just be, it's easy to see if our current being is aligned with our highest being.

Only then can we truly hold ourselves accountable for embodying our highest selves. Are you reacting from a place

RISE: A CALL TO THE LIGHT TRIBE

of emotion, or responding from a place of wisdom, love, and compassion? Do your actions speak to the essence of your spirit? Integrity and moral courage flow from spiritual accountability.

Sometimes, we do the bad things because they are easier than the good things. Yet, when we are firmly grounded in ourselves, connected to our truest selves and to all there is, it becomes easier to do the hard but worthwhile things. Cultivate your own ferocity. The time is now to conquer ourselves so that we can get out of our own way. And so, I call upon you to look around, then look inward, because there is much work to be done. The great work ahead is simultaneously that of helping New Earth emerge from the ashes of the old as we ourselves rise as beings of light.

What does this look like? It looks like someone who realizes their power. It looks like someone who is kind first and foremost to themselves, both in traditionally kind ways and also in ways more akin to a stern parent. It looks like someone who moves through the world with a deep understanding that separation from source is nothing more than evolution at work; Light knows itself better when it can experience all of the colors that comprise it and when it can see itself contrasted by darkness. It is thus someone who sees every living being as a brother or sister, and works in big and small ways—to the extent of their ability—to extend compassion and eliminate suffering anywhere they can.

This is living as spirit—diving headfirst into the abyss with unflinching love. As black is the absence of light, we must shine our light everywhere. How deeply will you dive? We are all really the same. Evil too comes from source. By seeing the divine in all, we give that which may not behave divinely the chance to choose a path of light.

When I call upon the light tribe to rise, I am calling upon you, along with every person who chooses to do the difficult work of

CHAPTER 11. THE GREAT WORK AHEAD

reconciling everything within them that is a reflection of the evils of the world. Evil exists out there because it exists within us too. The same applies to goodness. We live in a collective construct, and we are all complicit to it. This is ultimately what free will is about. Will you choose to walk in light, by illuminating the darkness everywhere so that it may be no more, and by moving past the labels, the stories, and thoughts of who you and others should be, into the truth of you and we all are?

I propose that in this holographic universe, we each as mirrors who hold within us the pattern of all that is, have the ability to change the universal blueprint.

The cosmic web—the largest scale view of our universe—is very reflective of the smallest scales we've been able to observe. The vast network of filaments that connects clusters of stars within galaxies and even galaxies themselves resemble the fascia that runs through our bodies.

Uncertainty and potential are fundamental building blocks of our reality. This story has been written, yes, but it's been written a zillion different ways, much like a pick-your-adventure novel where multiple outcomes have been written but not yet experienced by the reader immersed in the story. We collectively get to decide the outcome we experience. In quantum mechanics, this is the Heisenberg principle of uncertainty at work.

Scientists have determined that in tiny amounts of time and space, something can come from the vacuum of nothing, nature's default state. The vacuum is actually alive with quantum-sized packets of light that quickly appear and disappear. Just as these packets appear, so do mirror images that are their anti-matter equivalent, anti-light, so to speak. So for every pinprick of light, there is a corresponding pinprick of darkness, perhaps akin to a tiny black hole.

RISE: A CALL TO THE LIGHT TRIBE

These opposite mirrors dance in space until colliding, annihilating each other almost instantly, because you can, according to physics, borrow energy from nothing if you pay the debt back quickly. But here is what I find most interesting about this quantum phenomenon: Although these opposite particles are mirror images of each other, when they collide into destruction, there is always just the tiniest bit left, but what remains is always of the light particle.

This is why everything we see exists, because light always remains. It always persists destruction. The universe sprang from the vacuum through the creation and annihilation of matter and anti-matter particles. The remaining matter, combined with the energy released from countless collisions birthed galaxies, and eventually, us.

The tangled dance between good and evil, light and dark, that we now see playing out in our reality is nothing more than a reflection of this quantum-scale activity. And thus, in the collision of duality, there is no question that light will persist, as it always has. The question that remains to be answered is just how much suffering will we allow ourselves to bear and bear witness to?

Every moment of every day, we pass critical choice points in this cosmic choose-your-adventure narrative. We all play a role in steering this ship, in co-choosing how this story turns out. I, for one, have had enough of the old narrative. It is thus my commitment to myself, to you, and to everything that is to engage in relentless self-inquiry, to look unflinchingly inward and outward at everything that is not light so as to illuminate and transmute it, and do take every opportunity upon which I come across to lead by example with compassion and integrity.

Put another way, this is living from a base level of love. In "Power vs. Force," Dr. David Hawkins wrote about what he calls the scale of consciousness, with a range of zero to 1,000.

CHAPTER 11. THE GREAT WORK AHEAD

Each step in the scale is associated with an emotion. At the very bottom are shame and guilt, with scores of 20 and 30, respectively. At the top of the scale is enlightenment, with a score of 700, and above that, pure Christ consciousness, at 1,000. Love sits at 500 on the scale.

Where someone or something sits on the scale can be determined, according to him, through muscle testing, because our bodies are intrinsically connected to the force field around us. According to this scale, anyone and anything that falls below 200—associated with courage—is a negative force, while anything above is a positive charge. Right around this critical point is where most of humanity sits. Yet, a single individual at a level of 500 can counterbalance and touch off change in as many as 750,000 individuals below the 200 line, according to Hawkins. The higher up you sit, the more impactful your mere presence in the world is. In other worlds, the ripples created by your drops upon the ocean travel farther.

Many people are saying this many different ways. So many of us are hearing the same messages, and feeling an urgency to share them. The drumbeat quickens. Timelines are accelerating and collapsing into one another, each passing moment eliminating options from the choose-your-adventure storyline. Both individually and collectively, we must shed all that no longer serves us, all that isn't in the highest vibration.

My friends, the time is now. What you came here to do is rise, so rise, however that looks for you. Gaia is counting on us, and the universe has our backs. We are the divine matrix; embodied beings of light co-creating a luminous reality. Never mind the flames all around us. We cannot be consumed. The phoenix rises.

The beginning is near.

About the Author

Cynthia Gomez is a lifelong student of soul science, the intersection of spirituality with every branch of knowledge. She blends spirituality, philosophy, and the sciences to help facilitate quantum healing and conscious living. She is a master life coach and is trained in Reiki and other intersectional energy work and meditative modalities. She is also a writer and spiritual entrepreneur. She hosts wholeness retreats through The Gaia Revolution. And through Light Rising Publishing and StoryTime Me, she offers unique publishing solutions to produce content that facilitates empowered personal storytelling, meaning-making, and wisdom sharing to ultimately expand consciousness and connectedness, and inspire kinder living.

www.ingramcontent.com/pod-product-compliance
Lightning Source LLC
Chambersburg PA
CBHW071003080526
44587CB00015B/2319